Knowing How

20 Concepts to Rewire the Brain

Knowing How

20 Concepts to Rewire the Brain

Julie Valenti

MANITOU
COMMUNICATIONS

Copyright © 2016 Manitou Communications, Inc.

1701 Gateway

Suite 349

Richardson, TX 75080

Phone: 972-918-9588

Fax: 972-918-9069

rossinst@rossinst.com

www.rossinst.com

Library of Congress Card Number: 2016947775

Valenti, Julie A.

Knowing How: 20 Concepts to Rewire the Brain

ISBN: 978-0-9815376-8-9

1. Childhood Trauma

Orders by U.S. trade bookstores and wholesalers. Please contact: Manitou Communications, Inc. Phone: 972-918-9588 Fax: 972-918-9069 or visit www.rossinst.com.

Printed in the United States of America

DEDICATION

We are all in this together.

This book is dedicated to all the survivors of child abuse, neglect and confusion. To those who are afflicted with Post Traumatic Stress Disorder originating in childhood and have used drugs, alcohol, sex, food, gambling and more to sooth and distract themselves from the pain of that disorder.

It is also dedicated to all the therapists, counselors, ministers, speakers, and writers who have committed their life's work to helping those who suffer.

And finally, this book is dedicated to the evolution of the human brain and body…Spirit and Soul.

WHAT PEOPLE ARE SAYING ABOUT THE 20 CONCEPTS

"The 20 Concepts helped me to change my patterns of self neglect and abuse learned in a dysfunctional childhood and repeated in adult relationships. Victim, abuser, and rescuer roles no longer have power over me. They are the perfect completion to my spiritual practice and my 12-Step work. I now live with happiness and awareness, using the tools that help me deal with the now-minor triggers in life."

– Neurologist Portland, Oregon

"The words that come to mind when I think about using the 20 Concepts are acceptance, compassion, and commitment, which I now have for myself and others. Julie provides simple, consistent concepts for growth and healing. It is a process that is centered in self-love and learning to harness the power and beauty in me. These lessons and techniques have changed the way I think and feel about many aspects of my life and have given me the courage to listen to my own voice. I am forever grateful."

– Realtor Portland, Oregon

"My wife and I used the Concepts during a difficult time in our marriage several years ago. We are still together 27 years now and our marriage has blossomed. These concepts really helped us communicate. I continue to encourage clients to use the 20 Concepts in my own practice."

– Naturopathic Doctor Vancouver, Washington

"The 20 Concepts saved my marriage, family, and sanity! They provided me with invaluable insights as to why I was reacting in certain ways and helped me break destructive patterns."

- Medical Doctor Portland, Oregon

"Using the 20 Concepts was hard, painful, and completely against all my instincts. Desperation brought me to Julie so I saw following the Concepts as my only hope; doing so has changed my life entirely for the best. My addictive behavior is beginning to seem like an alien part of my past and my relationships with my mom, husband, brother, friends, and coworkers have benefited."

– Executive Assistant Portland, Oregon

"Julie has made such an impact on my life and has touched the lives of so many with her gift to aid in healing the broken parts of our psyche; whether shattered as small children, smashed as adults, or fractured throughout the way...Julie has dedicated her life to helping others pick up the pieces; gain an understanding of how they were broken, and then shows how to put them back together in a way that really works. By teaching folks the very tools of how to heal their lives, they are given the incredible opportunity to go on and live the authentic, abundant life that each one of us was intended to live...with integrity, freedom from the traumas of the past, and with a more conscious, balanced mind. I recommend Julie and the 20 Concepts to anyone and everyone who comments on how many positive changes I've made or how much happier I am. She truly is a fantastic lady who shares her gift of love and wisdom with others through her work. I am eternally grateful."

- Hypnotherapist and Life Coach Wilsonville, OR

ABOUT THE AUTHOR

Julie Valenti

Over the past three and a half decades Julie has been passionately involved in the healing field; first as a Licensed Nurse and then as an Addictions Counselor. She became a Certified Hypnotherapist where she developed a deep understanding of the conscious and subconscious mind. Julie studied at the Ross Institute for psychological trauma to further her knowledge-base regarding childhood trauma and what devastating results there can be. She later became an ordained minister and performs marriage ceremonies as well as the sacred end-of-life rituals.

Julie is an avid and voracious researcher; always wanting to be on the "cutting edge" of new findings in the field of psychology, physiology, philosophy and physics. She does this to be the very best she can be when guiding, supporting and helping others on their journey. She is a survivor of childhood abuse and neglect and has been in ongoing recovery for over 30 years. Her life is dedicated to sharing her experience, strength and hope!

ACKNOWLEDGMENTS

With Heartfelt Gratitude

There are several people who I want to express my appreciation to and yet I struggle to find the words to articulate just how much each and every one of you mean to me:

Colin Ross – I will do my best to tell you, how much you have helped me by being my friend and mentor over the past ten years. After I shared the 20 Concepts with you over a decade ago you said four small but very powerful words to me; "You really get it!" Those words that have not only sustained me but motivated me to write this book. That belief in me, coming from such an accomplished man and one who has helped so many who suffer, meant the world to me and I am filled with pride to call you my friend!

Kathleen Cavanaugh, my editor, writing coach, and dear friend – You have supported me in ways that I cannot even begin to describe. Your hours of meticulous editing, along with your availability to talk me through the most difficult blocks is what has made my passion to write about this work transcend from my mind to the book we now hold in our hands.

Ronni, my sister and owner of Valenti Design – I want to express my ongoing gratitude for creating such a beautiful book design for Knowing How and for all the design and editing work you have done for the Wisdom and Recovery Wellness Center.

Molly Crawley, my soul friend – You have supported me from the beginning by editing my original book proposal. Having you champion and believe in me, and my work has been absolutely invaluable.

Sebastian and Adrian, my two sons – You have both believed in me and cheered me on during every phase of my career. Thanks for helping me set up and break down for my classes and workshops as well as helping me to navigate the technology that continues to baffle me.

A special thanks to all **my clients** who have used The 20 Concepts to change their lives; who have included me in their amazing process, and who insisted that I write this book so we could make Knowing How available to their families and friends.

And finally…**Randy** (wherever you are). You had the guts to challenge me, which in turn motivated me to create an approach to recovery that included the missing piece…Knowing HOW!!

DISCLAIMER

Proceed mindfully...

Knowing How: The 20 Concepts, is not intended to be a substitute for professional advice, diagnosis, medical treatment, or therapy. Always seek the advice of your physician or qualified mental health provider with any questions you may have regarding any mental health symptom or medical condition. Never disregard professional, psychological, or medical advice; nor delay in seeking professional advice or treatment.

CONTENTS

TABLE OF CONTENTS

FORWARD

The 20 Concepts are a very useful addition to the field of psychotherapy. Julie Valenti has been working on developing and refining the 20 Concepts for a decade, and has done an excellent job of distilling them into an easily understood set of principles. She has adapted, and expanded upon, the strategies and techniques of my Trauma Model Therapy for use in private practice, and has designed an outpatient treatment program that makes use of her approach.

I remember when I was a psychiatric resident, back in the days of chalk and chalk boards, sitting in a seminar on family systems theories. There were fourteen or fifteen different schools of family therapy listed on the board. Even though the lecturer went over them all one by one, there was no way I could actually remember them all, keep them separate in my mind, and apply them in clinical practice. I decided right then that if I ever wrote about psychotherapy in the future, or taught it in workshops, I would boil things down to some basic ideas that therapists could actually remember and use.

My Trauma Model Therapy is based on five core principles: the problem of attachment to the perpetrator; the locus of control shift; just say 'no' to drugs; addiction is the opposite of desensitization; and the victim-rescuer-perpetrator triangle. The locus of control shift is derived from family systems theory, which I found very interesting as a resident; the basic idea is that symptoms, diagnoses, addictions, and self-defeating behaviors are the solution to a problem in the background. The challenge for the therapist is to figure out what problem in the background is being solved by the presenting symptom(s) or behavior, and to help the person, or family, find a healthier way of solving the problem. Once the problem in the background is solved, it becomes easier to let go of the presenting addiction or behavior.

I believe that writing up a psychiatric history should be similar to writing a non-fiction short story about the person's life. Symptoms and diagnoses are embedded in a life story. They have a context, a meaning, and a purpose, and are part of a survival strategy. They can be unhealthy and self-defeating, but mental disorders and addictions aren't just a problem of "brain disease," as we are told by biological psychiatry. The life story approach is the foundation of the 20 Concepts, which is what gives them their therapeutic power.

In this book, Julie Valenti provides a practical, sensible set of principles for recovery from mental disorders, addictions, relationship problems, and life problems in general. She provides specific therapeutic tasks in the form of questions at the end of each chapter, so that the reader knows what to work on, and how to work on it, in a defined fashion. Julie's treatment model is technically eclectic – the more tools in the toolbox, the better – but it is conceptually and procedurally organized into an integrated series of recovery exercises. I am very pleased that Julie has adapted and expanded upon my Trauma Model Therapy, and has included an understandable explanation of neurophysiology in the 20 Concepts. I look forward to incorporating the 20 Concepts into my hospital-based Trauma Programs.

Colin A. Ross, M.D.
President and Founder of the Ross Institute for Psychological Trauma

ONE

Introduction

COULD I HAVE PTSD AND NOT KNOW IT?

How many times have you heard yourself say, "I *knew better* than to do that." and yet beyond all logic and reasoning, you did it anyway? It is said that our subconscious brain determines 88% of all we do, leaving only 12% of our behavior directed by the conscious, rational and logical part of our brain. How can this be true? In our world of highly technological functioning are we still operating with a brain that is hard wired for basic survival? How much *has* our brain evolved? How much have we as a people evolved? How happy are we, really? Is there something in our subconscious, some belief, some memory that drives us to sabotage the goals we have for our lives? These seem to be questions that many people are asking and if they are not, they should.

The population that is most severely affected by the often hidden workings of the subconscious mind; 3 million cases per year in the US, is those that have moderate to severe PTSD (Post Traumatic Stress Disorder) stemming from early childhood attachment conflicts and/or a traumatic life event. Many people are unaware that they have a form of PTSD and that this could be what is at the root of their conflicted relationships. Most of us, when we hear PTSD, immediately think it is only relevant to war veterans or survivors of some other extreme life-threatening situation. We are unlikely to realize how very fragile we are as children and how literally dependent we are on our caregivers for our lives.

As children, we know instinctively that we *must* attach to survive. When our attachment is compromised due to the unavailability of our caregivers, for whatever reason, it is experienced as a survival risk, causing traumatic stress. Faced with a survival threat, the child desperately creates strategies to feel safe. The strategies we develop become hardwired in the brain in an area where memory is stored. Due to the traumatic stress of the inability to securely attach and bond as a child, a healthy, secure attachment later in an adult intimate relationship is nearly impossible. Attempting to create that relationship can trigger our behavior into a childlike state resulting in immature responses and poor conflict resolution. We will cry, yell, strike out and/or run away if there are conflicts (which there will be) within the relationship. Running away as an adult often looks like alcohol or drug addiction. Other areas to run and hide can be work, food, and sex to name a few. These forms of "tuning out" that work best often become addictions.

There has been a lot of focus over the last 15 years on neuroplasticity, which simply put means we have the ability to rewire our brains. *Knowing How: The 20 Concepts* teaches us that, when used repeatedly, these Concepts can accomplish that rewiring.

These concepts can do for PTSD what the 12-Steps have done for alcoholism and addiction. In much the same way as the 12-Steps, The 20 Concepts must be studied, learned, spoken about and integrated into memory, and therefore our lives. Addicts and alcoholics have rewired their brains to use the 12-Steps in "all of their affairs." When triggered, remembering a step or slogan "re-minds" them that there is a different way to cope, in place of drinking or using. The 20 Concepts are a map of where to go when the PTSD person is triggered.

Due to 12-Step programs, the world is a safer place with less intoxicated and mood altered people driving cars, raising children, performing surgeries and so on. Similarly, our world will be a healthier and more peaceful place when people with PTSD are more awake, aware and conscious of the choices they make, instead of operating from a triggered, childlike survival position. We will then make better parents, teachers, leaders and humanitarians.

Untreated PTSD grows like a cancer; it affects everyone it comes in contact with. Parents with this disorder are also unavailable attachment figures and are raising children who have little hope of forming healthy relationships as adults. We have evolved in our medical science and found cures for many diseases that would disable a person or end his/ her life prematurely. Are we not capable of creating a cure for PTSD and finally putting an end to child abuse and neglect? Using The 20 Concepts whenever we are triggered or conflicted creates more activity in the creative/thinking part of the brain and less in the survival reactionary part; resulting in a more highly evolved and intelligent life. The rewiring process does work.

TWO

Randy and I

RANDY AND I

Randy entered my office in distress from debilitating anxiety and periods of deep, dark depression. He was in recovery from substance abuse and after several years of being clean and sober, he reported that he was still plagued with paralyzing fear, conflicted relationships and self-hatred. In moments of desperation he'd contemplate suicide, but stated that fortunately the thought of that option shook him to the core. I was in private practice at the time as an addictions counselor and began to examine his childhood to see if something had happened that might explain why Randy continued to return to a state of fear, conflicted attachments, and a sense of loss of self. In the addiction field this childhood exploration is called "family of origin work." Randy's parents drank and used drugs heavily which resulted in his ongoing abuse and neglect. They were also emotionally (and sexually) abusive towards him and each other.

After an extensive overview of Randy's childhood, I came to understand that he had PTSD due to his inability to attach securely as a child; this is where the real problem began for him. Many therapists and researchers often refer to these attachment conflicts as childhood trauma. I couldn't agree more. The trauma, in this case, is the inability to secure a lasting attachment (a loving, consistent feeling of safety and security,) thereby threatening the survival of the child. A child instinctively knows that attachment is necessary for survival. There is no decision made by the child, as it is a biological drive.

The trauma results when there is an inability to secure that bonded attachment, creating an overabundance of stress hormones in the brain and body, which then interferes with his or her healthy development on multiple levels. This will be explained in more detail later in this book. Abuse, neglect, inconsistency, loss of a parent; all of these and more can create that insecure attachment. Randy, now in his 30s, has what we call "hard-wiring" in his brain (memory) influencing the perception of his world as unsafe and his behavior looks like that of a victim, a helpless child who is unable to make choices. Sometimes his behavior reflected that of an abuser or perpetrator striking out with words and fists. He was also forever searching for a rescuer — someone or something that would take away the pain and confusion he experienced. All of this wiring was held deep in his subconscious brain and it was *this* memory that got stimulated again and again by the current events, causing him to regress to a childlike state of mind and his choices reflected that dynamic.

As Randy spoke of current difficulties in regard to his intimate relationships and work environment, I wondered, was it his memory influencing him to repeatedly re-enact the same drama and trauma that he had experienced as a child? The players and situations were different but the same attachment conflicts and feelings of fear and loss were present. The question was *why* Randy's memory caused him to seek out and repeat painful events from the past. The answer will become increasingly obvious as we understand the brain a little more clearly and its number one purpose…Survival.

Through our work together, Randy came to understand that, due to his parents' neglect and abuse, his perception of himself was one that he was "bad" and "wrong". He also understood that the way he behaved in intimate relationships was very close to the way his parents behaved with each other. Randy learned quickly that there were many options for living life and experiencing himself differently, yet he continued to find himself back in a place of regret, remorse and shame over his most recent self-deprecating thought or aggressive, fear-based action.

During Randy's next scheduled session he said something that changed the course of my work (and life) forever. He said that I had helped him to understand himself, why he made the choices he did, and he appreciated all the new healthy options that were available to him. Now that he understood the *why*, he wanted me to teach him *how* to consistently use those healthy options. He wanted to know how to make those "better" choices during the moments of fear, pain and confusion, which often had the potential to turn into day or week long bouts of despair due to his current mode of operation.

He wanted me to teach him *how* to have access to all those healthy choices *while* he was overwhelmed with feelings, which was exactly when he needed those skills to be readily available to him. At this point I came to the realization that I was not able to teach him these tools because I did not yet know how or in what way to explain them. The "Just do it" method seemed ridiculous in this situation yet there was little else readily available.

None of my psychological studies, addiction, and hypnotherapy certifications or medical training provided the information that was so vital to *lasting* change. I came to realize that retraining or rewiring the brain, clearly had to be the answer. *This* was the missing piece for people who enter therapy and the clients in my practice continue to confirm it time and time again.

Most people who walk through my door have been to several therapists. They have been involved in the 12-Step recovery program and/or read many "self-help" books. Yet, their lives, while improving on some levels, still contained confused and conflicted relationships with others and with themselves. They were hurting, angry and afraid because they were not yet living the life that they wanted for themselves

I have Dyslexia and have found that while this appeared to be a curse; it has actually been a blessing. As a result of my own struggle with learning, I have become an expert at creating systems for organizing complex strategies into the most simple and user-friendly steps. I realized that this was the only way I could absorb and retain information. I knew I could use this same systematic approach to teach Randy and all of my clients how to rewire their brains. The goal was to move from intense feelings quickly over to thought processes that would provide logical and reasonable strategies to resolve conflicted situations. Many of us know "logically" what to do, and now by learning this step-by-step approach we will know *how* to apply it!

You can and will learn how to re-wire your brain by creating rapid-firing neurological connections from the limbic system (feeling part of the brain) to the cerebral cortex (thinking part of the brain). Once you have established those pathways and strengthened them, through time and repetition, you will change the way you perceive the world. Your responses to all situations will be the way you want them to be rather than just utilizing the previous survival wiring, most of which was established in your childhood.

While creating this rewiring approach, I was first able to apply it in my own life and I was amazed by the changes that occurred. The integration of The 20 Concepts changed my life in the most profound ways. Whenever I experienced conflict in my life I thought of which concept to use to navigate the situation. There were always one or two that fit and by using them I had immediate relief and felt centered. Using this approach, after a period of time, I realized that I no longer had to search for the appropriate concept. My responses to life's challenging situations became automatic and effortless. The rewiring had taken place! Once these changes began to occur I realized what a tremendous, life-changing system I had developed, so I began to teach The 20 Concepts to my clients. The incredible feedback I have consistently received from them has only reaffirmed what I had already experienced in my own life and strengthened my resolve to spread the word.

Because of this work, my clients will tell you that their lives have been changed forever. They are happier and more peaceful than they've ever been; their relationships with others have improved; they themselves have more confidence and self-acceptance; and many of the long-lasting issues they have struggled with for years now have a solution for permanent change. They questioned why no other therapist, group or book taught them how to create permanent change in such a methodical and conscious way. Many commented that I should write a book so that The 20 Concepts could be available to help countless others who continue to struggle.

After Randy's bold request in the late 90's, I began to create a platform on which this rewiring approach could stand solidly. My passion was to research and understand one of the most significant systems at the core of our entire existence. That system is our human brain and body. Along with the most recent research and findings regarding brain science, specifically neuroplasticity, and building on my previous knowledge gained from my 10-year career in the medical field, I reviewed the workings of human anatomy and physiology; this helped me to understand the brain from an attachment and trauma perspective.

I also began to work toward my certification as a hypnotherapist. Hypnotherapy has taught me about the differences between the conscious and the subconscious parts of the brain. I learned how we can manipulate the neurological and hormonal wiring of the subconscious brain by using visualization. Visualizing (the imagining and picturing) of a healthy and functional life while in a deeply relaxed state influences hormonal responses in the body, creating a joyful and peaceful mood state, which then results in a physiological reaction through the entire organism.

Profound healing can happen using this technique. With repeated visualizing of positive choices and behaviors we create what we call, a memory. Another way of stating that is to say, the continuous activating of certain neuropathways in the brain creates patterns; when these patterns are established and used often, they become easy to utilize again and again in most situations. Most of us have heard the statement, "Neurons that fire together wire together"; this is basically how memory is created. Again, because of my learning disorder I had to break down this information into an approach that was simple and easy to utilize. Through understanding and repeated use of The 20 Concepts, I created positive results that were nothing short of amazing.

THREE

My PTSD and Rewiring

MY PTSD AND REWIRING

My career path began while I was still in my mother's womb. She was in her mid-20s, steeped in her addiction and overwhelmed with her unmanageable life. Her addiction began with the birth of her first child, my brother. In the 50's it was a common medical practice for physicians to prescribe amphetamines to new moms for quick weight loss and extra energy to help with sleep deprivation, due to middle of the night feedings that newborns require.

My mother came from a family with alcohol addiction. The abuse and neglect she experienced in that family resulted in her PTSD. As with many sufferers, the drugs were a quick and easy solution to the pain of this disorder. Once my mom had amphetamines in her system, she felt more powerful and capable than she ever had before and she quickly became addicted.

As with most drugs, she developed a tolerance to them and she required more and more to get the same result. Since amphetamines are a controlled substance, she would consistently run out of her pills before her pharmacy could legally provide a refill. Her days of waiting to get her prescription filled were laden with fits of anger and rage along with deep depression, muscle cramps and unconscious states. All of this created an inconsistent and confusing environment for my brother and later for me as well. When my mother had her pills she was delightful and when she ran out of them she was verbally and physically abusive. By the time my sister was born 8-years later, my brother's life had become one of ongoing abuse, neglect and confusion.

Being a small child and not having the vocabulary to express his fears, wants and needs, my brother would act-out his feelings. My sister's birth gave my mother the daughter that she wanted so desperately. Neither of my parents expected that I would be conceived only 9-months later. Tragically, for all of us in that family, my mother didn't stop her abuse of amphetamines until almost 20 years after my birth.

I remember as a young child hearing my mother calling out in the middle of the night in despair and how I would run to her bedside (or wherever I might find her) to soothe her. I'd rub her cramping legs or help her off the floor into bed or a chair. I became her personal savior. To her, I was the only one who loved and understood her. She had alienated my father, my sister, and my brother. I became "hers" instead of myself. Later in life my sister would bitterly accuse me of being "Mom's favorite". She could never understand the price I paid for that position.

Few people understand the deep wound of loss-of-self unless they look at the ways in which they too have lost large parts of themselves, in a desperate subconscious attempt to form and keep an attachment figure, regardless of how unhealthy. In the past I would reenact the *Victim/ Perpetrator/Rescuer* dynamic (more about this in Concept 3) in my own life with ongoing drug and alcohol abuse and the attachment to partners who were also abusive. The pain of this would occasionally bring me to the point of considering the option of suicide for pain relief, as Randy once did.

At age 18, I married my first drug addict. But truth be told, I had begun rescuing the drug addict, the sick and the needy many years prior, first with my mother and then my sister. My father, who also had an alcoholic father and abusive mother, became emotionally and often physically absent. Today, my brother continues the pattern of the victim/perpetrator in his own adult life. Sadly, his children also followed that pattern.

My parents went to an early grave as a result of the physical and emotional abuse and neglect that they perpetuated in their own lives. My parents smoked, ate poorly, never exercised and refused to implement any healthier behaviors into their lives; like so many who still suffer with PTSD, even though they "knew better" they still did not possess the tools or the belief that it was possible to change. My mom died of diabetes and my dad of lung cancer. I have a saying, "First at the hands of others and then at my own," which simply means we will continue to repeat the patterns we acquired from our most impressionable years unless we learn a new way. We will often end up hurting ourselves in much the same way we were affected as children.

After a painful marriage and divorce of my first alcohol and drug-addicted husband, I entered into the nursing field. It was another subconscious attempt to reenact that which I had learned in my childhood so that I could maintain my identity. In my memory, I was one who helps the sick and this was how I could matter, be loved and safe. The wiring was deeply established. I also had a series of relationships with lovers and friends that abused drugs consistently and I was using right along with them. I married my second husband, also a heavy alcoholic and drug user, while deep in my own addictive and reenacting life.

The distress of this relationship combined with the preceding trauma had brought me to my knees. A close friend and coworker at the hospital I was working at suggested I attend an Al-Anon meeting; I took his advice and sought help for myself. I could no longer deny the pattern I had repeated since childhood of attaching to the sick, the helpless, and the addicted. I brokenheartedly left my second husband, when he refused to stop drinking. I returned to school to try to understand addiction and later graduated from JFK University of Psychology in the San Francisco Bay area, as an Addictions Counselor. Along with this tremendous knowledge base and the implementation of the tools of the 12-Step recovery programs, one might think my reenactment ended there. But, like Randy, I still didn't know how to change the deep patterns in my brain of rescuing and these patterns once activated, determined my choices and behavior in spite of all my logic and reasoning.

My third husband was my supervisor at the drug and alcohol treatment hospital where I was an intern. He was a 3-year recovering heroin user and had two master degrees in psychology. He eventually obtained his PhD yet, was also unable to change his own hardwired patterns - even with his amazing education he acted out his addicted behavior in a multitude of ways. I now look back on his childhood to make sense of his behavior. Even though he was smart enough to know that the events of his childhood were driving his behavior, he could not seem to control it. We were together for 10 years and had two beautiful sons, yet I was dying inside. I was dying a slow death from recreating a life where I was consistently trying to fix my attachment figure, thereby abandoning and neglecting the little lost self that was inside of me. This pattern was all too familiar.

Two years after our divorce I began my work with Randy. The approach I created as a result of that interaction, and the subsequent research, both professional and personal, resulted in a philosophy that I embrace in my life and my life's work today. I live consciously, creatively, joyfully and full of adventure. I no longer find my value in rescuing and fixing. I have a deep sense of trust in myself and have found peace. I never saw Randy again and do not know to this day what ever happened to him. I think of him often and hope the best for him. He started me on this amazing journey and now The 20 Concepts have changed the lives of hundreds of others in profoundly positive ways. And now, if you are ready, willing and committed, the use of The 20 Concepts can change yours.

FOUR

The 20 Concepts

This section of the book explains each one of The 20 Concepts. At the end of each concept description, there will be several questions for you to ask yourself. I highly recommend hand writing the answers and even more helpful, that you create a journal and write about what memories, thoughts and feelings each concept (and the questions) bring up for you. This is the beginning of the rewiring process, which will be explained in more detail in the How to Re-wire chapter, later in the book.

CONCEPT 1

Understanding Your Brain and Body

Understanding Your Brain and Body

Before we can attempt to re-wire our brain and body we must understand its working parts, as well as how we are currently wired. While all brains have a similar shape, size and function, wiring is unique to each person and is based on genetics, and environment. There is an ongoing debate in the field of psychology which is: whether the make-up of who and how we are is primarily a result of *nature*, meaning our DNA and what happens while we are still in our mother's womb; or *nurture*, meaning the involvement of our caregivers and the environment in which we are raised. The most effective viewpoint is to understand that *identity* comes from neither one nor the other, but that both contribute significantly to how our brain and body is wired.

Nature is where development begins. Our wiring process starts while we are in the womb and attached to our mother through our umbilical cord. The mother, in addition to the feeding of nutrients, is supplying other substances to the fetus, such as various hormones. Most of us are familiar with the negative effects of drug or alcohol consumption during pregnancy and the recommendation of a healthy diet and daily exercise. Not as many of us understand that the emotional state of the mother is just as important to the fetus's healthy development. For example: If the mother is anxious and has large amounts of stress hormones in her system such as adrenaline and/or cortisol, those hormones will be delivered to the fetus. Does that mean that an anxious mother results in an anxious baby? The answer is yes, absolutely! Therefore part of understanding our neurological wiring is researching what was going on emotionally with our mother while we were in the womb.

Now let's look at *nurture*, which is the relationship we have with our caregivers and the environment we were raised in as children. The ideal environment is one where the home is consistently and predictably safe, and all basic survival needs are being met. Are you aware that a basic need for survival is to be touched, held, and interacted with? As a baby we need parents who are available to touch, cuddle and hold us. We are a species that are hard wired to attach and bond for survival. If an infant is not touched the baby could very likely develop failure to thrive, be sickly and or even die. We also need caregivers that are involved with us, that are encouraging, supporting and validating. This includes how parents relate to each other. Parents who demonstrate love for each other, that are playful, respectful and loving to each other help a child to develop stress-free. They also assist the child in learning behaviors and principles regarding what a healthy, loving couple and family look like.

If a child is raised in an environment where there is violence, neglect, confusion or abuse, that child will likely have an overabundance of stress hormones activated by fear. The child, on a subconscious level, processes the situation of two angry or absent caregivers as a potential threat to survival. If this stressful situation is the norm, over time this child's baseline hormonal balance will be that of high adrenaline and cortisol. These are fight or flight hormones that prepare the body for action and because little children cannot fight or flee (run away), the hormones are not utilized and discharged from the body through these actions. The consequences of this overload of stress hormones can be a multitude of problems.

Some researchers say that children who are raised in an environment of high stress, whether due to abuse or neglect, have a higher chance of developing a learning disorder. It is reported this can be due to high levels of the stress hormone cortisol, which causes damage to the fragile wiring of a child. Children raised in a stressful environment will also have a tendency to develop anxiety disorders, depression, addictions, alcoholism and/or other mental disorders as adults. Many will have PTSD and will easily be triggered into a state of fear by loud voices, angry facial expressions or when someone leaves or rejects them. Once we reach the age of approximately 25, it is said we are hard-wired.

This may be a good place to mention that as small children our ability to fully process complicated situations is undeveloped; such as any type of instability in our parents and/or their tendency to act out through purposefully or inadvertently harming or neglecting us. Our cerebral cortex and prefrontal lobes are underdeveloped and as mentioned will not be fully wired until our mid-twenties. When abuse or neglect happens during childhood, we have the experience and feeling, but no logical thought about it. This is not only due to the underdeveloped thinking brain, but also because when our fight or flight hormones are activated due to stress, the thinking part of the brain decreases in activity while the emotional and hormonal part of the brain increases in activity. This partially explains why adults who come to see me say things like, "I didn't *think* my parents were abusive or neglectful", even while reporting experiences that indicate otherwise.

There are two areas of the brain we need to familiarize ourselves with: The conscious part and the subconscious part. Remember in an earlier chapter the statistic that 88% of all we do is subconscious (feeling/memory) and only 12% is conscious thinking. It's important we understand why those numbers seem to be so out of balance. We will begin with examining the subconscious part of the brain because it is the first area to develop. One part of our subconscious brain is responsible for regulating all our bodily functions which involves our body temperature, immune system, heart rate and circulation; respirations, digestion, reproductive organs, and hormonal production and activation; all of these systems work together to keep the body alive.

Another part of our subconscious brain is called the limbic system, which is occasionally referred to as the "seat of emotion". Memory storage is also a function of the limbic part of the brain. We have 5 senses: smell, sight, touch, hearing, and taste, which are constantly informing the body of the environment. The limbic section of the brain has the job of determining if what is happening is good for survival or not. This data is stored in memory for immediate access, which will determine what our behavior will be in any given situation.

Let's look more closely at emotion. What exactly are emotions? Are emotions the same as feelings? If you remember back to high school biology, we all learned about atoms and molecules and that our bodies are filled with energy. Well, some of that energy movement has to do with nerve impulses activated by the senses, which then stimulate hormonal secretion. We have many different hormones and the ones we will focus on are: 1. Stress hormones (fight or flight) such as adrenaline and cortisol; 2. Feel good hormones such as serotonin, endorphins and dopamine; and; 3. Sex hormones such as oxytocin, testosterone, and estrogen. There are hundreds of hormones and the ones I listed are not exclusive to these functions. For example testosterone can also be utilized as a stress hormone as it is a very aggressive one.

So back to the question, are emotions the same as feelings? E-motion or energy in motion *is* the same as feelings. I'll explain… When one of our senses gets stimulated, nerves are activated and they stimulate a particular endocrine gland, which houses our hormones. These glands are located throughout the body. Once a gland is stimulated it secretes the correct hormone or a combination of hormones into the blood system, which then prepares the body to take action. The reason we call this activity "feeling" is because we can *feel* it. Think about our heart pounding when we are frightened or a "gut feeling" when something seems wrong. These are a couple of examples of nerve/hormonal activity that we can *feel*. I will talk more about this later, but for now it's important to remember that our subconscious brain is our survival brain. It is responsible for all of our bodily functions including emotions, our memory, and our actions in external situations.

Next, we look at the conscious brain, also known as our cerebral brain. This part of the brain is responsible for logic, reasoning, formulas and all thinking. We do not need this part of the brain for basic survival; however it has become a vitally important component of living a highly functional life in today's evolved world. It is also said that the conscious brain is our creative brain. Simply explained, first we must think of something in order to create that something. Just look around you at all the manufactured or created things in your environment. Wouldn't you agree that at first, all these things were created from someone's thought or idea? The computer where I write was first someone's thought; as was my iPhone; this desk where I sit, as well as the chair I am currently sitting on. The conscious brain is indeed our creative brain!

The conscious thinking and subconscious survival are often communicating with each other. For example, if you feel hungry, you might think, "What shall I eat?" Or if you feel tired, you may think, "Maybe I'll go to sleep soon." However, if you feel fear, anger or any other stimulation of stress hormones, the activity in the thinking part of your brain would decrease and the activity in your survival brain would increase. Because your body is activated by fight or flight hormones, your behavior would be to automatically strike out or get away. We might not only fight by striking out physically, we might yell or scream. We also might go to flight by disassociating or refusing to speak.

These behaviors are typically automatic and there is no real thought involved. Again, once the activation of survival hormones takes place, our thinking brain shuts off because it's time for action.

The brain's primary purpose is to keep the body (organism) alive, so by the time you are in your mid-twenties it has hardwired and holds in memory what to do to achieve that task of survival. If you are alive—and you are if you are reading this—your brain wants you to attach to people that are similar to your original attachment figures. You will also want to create similar dynamics, ones that are familiar to you. In addition, where your brain is concerned *known* or *similar* means safety and little or no threat. The brain is not so focused on your pleasure as it is on survival. It doesn't want you to start doing things differently because the unknown poses as a survival threat. This again, is referred to as "hard-wiring."

By now it's becoming more obvious why the subconscious is responsible for such a large percentage of what we do. Yet, when we take a look at the conscious or "thinking brain" and how very powerful it is, can we successfully increase its activity, thereby creating a more satisfying life? The answer is yes! This will require a rewiring process, which we now know is possible, thanks to the advances in neuroscience! No longer just a theory, but indeed, a fact. Neuroplasticity and rewiring is an absolute possibility!

ASK YOURSELF

What was going on in my mother's life while I was in her womb?

What were my parents' childhoods like?

When I was a small child, was my mother stressed or happy and well adjusted? How about my father?

What am I holding in memory about my childhood experiences?

Was I held and touched?

Was I hit, grabbed or yelled at?

How important did I feel?

Continue to explore:

Were both my parents involved in my life?

In what ways am I like and unlike my childhood attachment figures?

Answering these questions honestly is the beginning of understanding both the genetic and emotional wiring of your brain and body.

CONCEPT 2

Attachment

Attachment

In order for a child to survive it must attach. If abandoned, the little organism will surely die. A child will do everything possible to maintain a secure attachment - this is instinctual. If the *attachment* figures are unavailable for *any* reason, it is experienced as a trauma because the brain registers it as "life-threatening." As a result, the child's brain/body becomes stressed. Since a child cannot fight or use flight, they must come up with other strategies to try to obtain attachment.

There are a multitude of reasons why the attachment figures in our lives might not be available. In my childhood my mother was addicted to amphetamines and my father was out trying to provide for our family. Whether it is an addiction to drugs, alcohol, workaholism, co-dependency, sex or any other substance or behavior, the attachment figure is unavailable for secure and healthy bonding. Another reason attachment could have been compromised would be if one or both of your caregivers had a mental disorder such as depression, bipolar, obsessive compulsive disorder or any other psychological condition.

Even if your attachment figure (or you or a sibling) was ill with frequent hospitalizations and/or there was ongoing separation from your parents, this also would cause an attachment disruption. If a parent dies, this most certainly and sadly would result in an attachment disorder. Once a client told me that when he was a small child his mother had died. His father was overcome with grief that he began drinking and could not be available to this small child. So in a way, the client lost his father too.

What about adoption? There seems to be a lot of research indicating that children who were adopted, often struggle with forming healthy attachments in adulthood. This makes sense when you think of the attachment of the fetus in its mother's womb. The baby is wiring up to her energetically and is holding in memory the way she moves, the sound of her heartbeat, the tonality of her voice. Upon birth the little organism is hardwired to re-attach to the same organism in which it was developing in, over the previous 9 months. When the infant is put directly into the hands of strangers an attachment trauma exists.

The findings regarding newborns and attachment were so significant that very few hospitals currently remove the baby from their mother immediately after birth, and nurseries filled with plastic beds and crying newborns are almost a thing of the past. The clients I see who were adopted are dealing with abandonment and/or dependency issues in intimate adult relationships. Many people who were adopted lived in one or more foster homes before finally being adopted. In those cases the attachment disruption can happen several times.

Lastly, looking at how attachment during childhood can be conflicted, we examine neglect and/or physical, emotional, or sexual abuse – and sometimes all of the above. Along with the attachment system in the brain is a recoil mechanism. This is a self-protecting system that alerts a child to withdraw from a painful situation - yet the attachment system will always override the impulse to recoil. Recoil is not a viable option for a small child, as only attachment ensures survival. A conflicted attachment in childhood, no matter the reason, will almost certainly result in attachment conflicts as an adult.

Here are a few examples of adult attachment-conflicted types:

The Dependent:

This is when a person develops a dependency to another. The relationship exists out of a *need* as opposed to a desire. There is an addictive quality to the union and any threat to the relationship ending can activate PTSD. When this happens the person who is experiencing the potential threat will regress to a childlike state and hold onto their partner as if their life depends on it. They will cry, yell, scream and use other kinds of childlike strategies to stay attached. Here we see the "need-to–attach-to-survive" memory pattern at play. I have seen many men and women put up with horrific physical and/or emotional abuse; as well as neglect due to drugs, alcohol, work, or affairs. They may try to leave, but find that they are driven to come back due to the obsessive/compulsive nature of addiction.

It is very difficult to have a partner that uses you as an addiction or that develops a dependency on you. There is a tendency to *feel* objectified and/or responsible for their happiness and it becomes an obligation. This puts a lot of strain on the relationship. Yet, chances are if you don't have your own attachment issues, you will leave this relationship. People with healthy and secure attachment styles do not stay with people who are acting out their own unhealthy ones.

The Ambivalent:

This looks exactly as you would think it would when one person is ambivalent about the relationship. They vacillate between thinking, "I really want this to work out and I really want to get away from it." Part of the problem here is that the brain is driven to bond and attach; yet the memory it holds is one that attachment hurts, thereby activating the recoil reaction. We see this when there is one person who seems to be sabotaging the health of the relationship. These couples break-up and make up again and again.

The Avoidant:

These are people you will meet who boast that they are a bona fide bachelor or bachelorette and the last thing they *want* is a partner to complicate their life. They may have short-term relationships, but after a while they begin to experience the feeling of being smothered or restricted (controlled) in some way. Again, attachment-memory, if painful, sends the message that it's safer to "not even go there", so-to-speak.

You can see that if someone with a dependent attachment style tries to attach to someone with an ambivalent or avoidant style that the relationship will be doomed to be miserable or end.

Attachment as an adult is no longer a necessity for survival and many single people have wonderful exciting lives. But if your longing for a relationship and find that you are relating to some of the attachment conflicts that you have just read about, you will want to ask yourself some important questions.

ASK YOURSELF

When I was a child, what made attachment difficult?

What did I do to try to get my caregivers to attach to me?

Did I abandon parts of myself and adopt behaviors to get my parent approval?

Is there still a part or parts of myself that I won't allow to be expressed?

As an adult, do I recognize any of the above mentioned attachment styles in myself?

If I'm in a relationship, do I recognize them in my partner?

Do I view being in a relationship as a need or as a desire?

Do I stay in relationships that are unhealthy?

CONCEPT 3

Victim/Perpetrator/Rescuer Triangle

Victim/Perpetrator/Rescuer Triangle

This is a dynamic that exists for children who are in homes with caregivers who are either unavailable or abusive in some way. These children are *victims* because they cannot stop the abuse; they are too small and helpless. Nor can they leave the home, as they would not be able to survive on their own. If the child is being neglected they will go to extreme lengths to get noticed. Sometimes they will be an overachiever or an underachiever. If one of the strategies doesn't work they will try another.

It is usually the parents who play the part of the *perpetrator* in the triangle. They are the abusers and/or the neglectful ones who cannot meet the child's needs. This is usually due to their own childhood needs not being met. The *rescuer* is someone who could help the child such as other family members, teachers, friends and/or neighbors. Yet, all too often there is no rescuer and the child is left hurt, confused and in need. Sometimes the child will switch from the victim role into the rescuer role and try to get their needs met by taking care of a sick or sad parent. As a last minute survival strategy and an effort to be noticed, perhaps the child who's being neglected might act out as a perpetrator causing trouble within the family. This unhealthy pattern will surely repeat itself in various ways, in our adult relationships.

The *Victim/Perpetrator/Rescuer Triangle* dynamic can get hardwired into the brain's memory and all of our adult conflicts can be seen through this lens. For example, if someone does something that we don't like, we can quickly see him or her as a perpetrator and ourselves as victims. The belief is that they did something to us. As a reactionary measure, we then can "get them back" by jumping over to the perpetrator point in the triangle, to do something harmful to them – trying to make them a victim to "see how *they* like it." We can act this out with partners, friends, bosses, co-workers and onward. Sometimes we will even see life's circumstances as a perpetrator and ourselves as the victim.

The rescuer can be anything from drugs, alcohol, an affair, to work, shopping and so forth; they don't only come in human form. If you were raised in a family where you took care of one of your attachment figures or siblings, then you may find that you are hardwired to be a rescuer. Teachers, nurses, doctors, therapists and many people in the "helping" profession had childhoods where they were rescuing to survive. Remember, earlier in this book, I wrote of how I attempted to rescue my mom over and over to get her to attach to me; then became a nurse? Eventually I began to gravitate toward partners who *needed* help. This is a completely ineffective way to live in the adult world because it is regressive and therefore, childlike.

Whenever we are having conflicts with people or situations, it is important to be sure we are not thinking we are the victims of another or of the circumstances. Once we are adults, we are no longer victims unless we are forced against our will to do something. We need to watch our behaviors making sure that we are not being harmful to anyone and we must not be acting in a co-dependent way by rescuing to get cared about or to feel valid. Codependency is being dependent on someone else's opinion of you to validate who you are to yourself. An example is, if someone tells you that you made a mistake you immediately think you are wrong, but if they say you are wonderful then you can be proud of who you are.

CONCEPT 3: VICTIM/PERPETRATOR/RESCUER TRIANGLE

Your identity is dependent upon another's opinion. Therefore, if you want to be seen as great and wonderful you will do all kinds of things for others, including allowing them to take advantage of you. Often people will use the term "people pleaser;" which is another way of exhibiting co-dependent behavior and therefore being a rescuer. As children we were dependent upon our parents to reflect back to us that we were valid and worthy, that we were good and that we mattered. This would have created a secure sense of self. Unfortunately, many of us didn't get that, and as a result we end up insecure and always looking for the approval of others.

The *Victim/Perpetrator/Rescuer Triangle* dynamic is hardwired into the brain's memory and gets acted out in adult relationships again and again until we change this wiring. When in conflict, be sure you are not seeing yourself or others from this triangulated viewpoint.

ASK YOURSELF

In what way was I a victim as a child?

Was I neglected or abused emotionally, physically or sexually?

Am I ready to accept that spanking, grabbing, slapping and other physical pain implemented by our parents or siblings was abuse?

Did I have a secure attachment to my caretakers?

Did I try to rescue (help) one or both of my parents? How about a sibling?

Do I understand the term co-dependency?

As an adult do I often see myself as a victim and others as perpetrators?

Do I experience myself as a people pleaser or am I trying to fix someone or some situation?

Am I willing to ask myself if I am playing one of the roles in the triangle when I am in conflict with someone?

What does the situation look like if I refuse to occupy a point in the triangle?

CONCEPT 4

Locus of Control

Locus of Control

Locus of Control is a vital stage in a child's development. The term simply means "the location of control." As a child's brain develops over the course of 25 years, the actual thinking part of the brain is the last to be wired; therefore the child constructs "beliefs" based on his or her experiences. Children believe that they make everything happen; beginning with their crying which typically gets their parents' attention. To a child this means, "I'm in control of what happens." The child's belief in making things happen is consistently reinforced from blowing out candles on a birthday cake in order to get their wish to come true to wishing on the first star in the sky.

Children believe that if they make good things happen then they also are making bad things happen. This is reinforced when parents tell the child that it is because they are bad that they are being hit, slapped, spanked or sent away to their rooms. Sometimes parents say things like, "You make me so angry!" "You make me sick", or "You make me drink, leave, cry and/or feel terrible!" Now the child believes that if the parents neglect or hurt him/her, it's not because the parents are bad or wrong, it's because *the child is*. Children also believe that they are responsible for their parents' fights, divorces and even deaths.

In adulthood we can have a deep subconscious *belief* that there is something wrong or bad about us. This is beyond logic and reasoning because it isn't in the thinking part of the brain! It is a belief that has been hard wired into the subconscious brain of a child and the child's identity has formed around it.

This belief can show up in a couple of different ways as an adult. One identifier is "The Imposter Syndrome" which at the core is the sense that there is something bad and wrong about me. Regardless of all that you have achieved, you still believe that any day someone will discover the truth – that you are "just faking it." I have heard this from attorneys, physicians and many other successful people. Another way we see this deep-rooted belief that there is something wrong about us is called "Self-Sabotaging Syndrome." These two identifiers can often be connected. After thinking over and over again that "I'm bad and wrong," our anxiety and/or depression increases. This eventually impedes our ability to perform (i.e., self-sabotage) and our internal reality begins to show up externally.

Adults often believe that they can get others to do things for them, which will "make them safe." Again, this is a childlike belief. It is up to us, as adults, to make ourselves safe; compulsively trying to control people and situations (which immaturely, we unrealistically believe we can) only to keep us stuck in a regressive place.

We can only control ourselves, and how we think, feel and behave. If we continue to believe that we make things happen we will stay embedded in "magical thinking" which is the thinking of a child; and as a result, our lives will look childlike.

ASK YOURSELF

Do I believe if I change, others will also?

Do I plan, plot or otherwise try to think of ways to get others to do what I want?

Do I believe that the right person will make me safe?

Do I assume responsibility for problems even when I know I did nothing wrong?

Regardless of all that I have achieved, do I still have a sense that there is something wrong with me?

Do I think I am an imposter and will at some point be found out?

Is there some self-sabotaging going on in my life?

Am I willing to embrace the truth that I can only control my thoughts, feelings and behaviors and no one else's?

CONCEPT 5

Magical Thinking

Magical Thinking

Children's brains are underdeveloped so they use strategies to get their needs met such as wishing and hoping – clearly, this is where we get the term "childlike". If the wish seemed to have worked on birthday cakes and stars in the sky, then it should work here, too. Children have wild imaginations and have the ability to pretend things are different in order to escape the truth of what is happening or not happening – especially in regards to the behavior of their parents and what home feels like day in and day out. Sometimes the fantasy of their make-believe world gets taken outside of the home and they can convince other people of a very different picture than what their home-life actually looks like.

As adults they can continue to create made-up stories to gain acceptance and/or the admiration of others. Some labels used for these people are compulsive or pathological liars. Magical thinking could even be the beginning of a disorder called DID (Dissociative Identity Disorder), formerly known as Multiple Personality Disorder. DID develops when a child uses his/her strategies to escape abuse or neglect and in doing so, creates more than one reality or personality.

Another one of the ways in which magical thinking is evident in adulthood is when someone continues to wish and hope for something to be different yet does nothing to try to create a difference; such as setting boundaries and limits for themselves and/or others. There is a quote by Einstein that is often used in the 12-Step community, which states, "The definition of insanity is doing the same thing over and over again and expecting a different result."

ASK YOURSELF

Do I find myself wishing or hoping things will get better or be diffcrent without actually "doing" anything to affect that change?

Do I deny the seriousness of a situation and *pretend* it's really not that bad?

Do I get lost in fantasy?

Do I find myself embellishing stories to make myself look better?

Do I omit and withhold information because I'm afraid someone might judge me?

Am I able to be honest with others and myself about who I am?

CONCEPT 6

Triggers to Regression

Triggers to Regression

This is where we begin to understand the origins and effects of PTSD. Any situation that externally activates one of the five senses: sight, sound, smell, touch, and taste, can cause a trigger. For example, the brain processes the sense of sound, first by checking with memory for recognition and asking, "Does this sound familiar?" If this is the case, the next question would be, "Is it dangerous?" For example, "Was this sound ever present when I experienced a threat to my survival?"

Remember, a threat to survival is when attachment in childhood was compromised by abuse, neglect or inconsistency. If the triggering was indeed present during a time of high stress and fear, a regressive state will occur. A regressive state involves hormonal activation, which is similar to what was happening when the survival threat first occurred.

A common example and one that most people can relate to is the story of the war veteran returning home from active duty. He might hold in his memory that his life was threatened frequently by enemy gunfire. Now, if he is walking down the street and hears a loud exhaust system backfire (the trigger) from a nearby car, his brain immediately registers the sound as one that was heard before during a real, life-threatening situation and instantaneously a regressive state follows. This regressive state means that his body and brain are reacting just as they did when he was in active combat; his stress hormones escalate preparing the body for action and he dives into the bushes to take cover, sweating and trembling; yet this man returned from the war five years ago and today, is perfectly safe. You may not be jumping into the bushes to take cover when you are triggered, but we all have our own story and different triggers; our reactions will likely be in direct proportion to our experiences and how they affected us, until we learn a different way to respond.

Recalling what we learned in *Concept 1: Understanding Your Brain and Body*, the limbic part of the brain (where memory and hormonal reactions occur) cannot differentiate between the past and the present; thus a dive into the bushes by a triggered war veteran is understandable. A triggered brain decreases activity in the logical and reasoning (conscious) part of the brain and activates the survival part along with the associated stress hormonal response. This is why the veteran reacted the way he did in the previous example.

The same set of PTSD systems get activated when we have experienced childhood trauma (or any perceived trauma) throughout our life. For example, we may have been raised by an angry, emotionally and/ or physically abusive parent. This is traumatizing to us because the very person we are trying to attach to is hurting us and compromising the attachment. As a result, the brain registers this lack of bonding as potentially life-threatening. Remember, as children, we must attach to our caregivers to survive.

Now, let's say in adulthood we are in a relationship with someone and that person begins to get angry, has an angry expression on his or her face and speaks to us using a loud voice. There is nothing wrong with that person expressing his or her feelings, nor is this likely to be life-threatening. Yet, our survival brain registers this occurrence as *close enough* to our childhood experience; when survival was potentially at risk.

The components of this experience as an adult will trigger the same stress hormones that were present during our abusive past, thereby activating similar feelings and behaviors as well - we may find ourselves crying, pouting, running away, yelling and screaming, hitting, cowering, etc. Intimate, adult relationships simulate parent-child bonding; there is cuddling, kissing, calling each other honey, baby or sweetie pie; therefore we may find that we are in a semi-triggered state already and it doesn't take much to activate a stress response. Often a negative tone-of-voice or a familiar expression of disapproval is enough to trigger us into a state of regression and immaturity. Remember, both logic and reasoning are unavailable when the survival (subconscious) part of the brain is activated. Post Traumatic Stress Disorder simply states that: *After the trauma is over, the stress response continues to be activated by a trigger and our lives and relationships may seem to have no logical or reasonable order.*

It is important as adults to know what external situations can trigger us. As previously stated in concept 1, we must be aware of and understand the sensations in our body and consciously *think* in order to keep activity in the cerebral cortex at the same time as we are having feelings. When we are having an emotional reaction to any given situation it is always a good idea to first take several deep breaths and ask ourselves, "What is happening and why do I feel the way I do?" before we speak or respond in any way. In the beginning of doing this work we will likely need to take a time out or temporarily walk away in order to think. One can almost always request to leave and use the restroom. Checking in with ourselves this way breaks the stimulation that caused the trigger, and allows us to ask ourselves the above questions. Consciously *thinking* reduces activity in the limbic survival part of the brain. Another good question to ask is, "Has anything like this happened in my childhood?"

In *Concept 15: Anchors to Triggers*, we will look at some other ways to keep ourselves from going into regressive states. We must have logic and reasoning with which to handle adult situations. With time and repetition, we are creating rapid-firing neuropathways from our survival brain to our thinking brain. We are then able to evolve into more intelligent human beings and our choices and behaviors will reflect that maturity. As a result, the trigger will no longer have the power to shut down activity in our thinking (conscious) brain and our choices and behaviors will reflect the current events that are *actually* taking place in our adult lives. Our lives can have order and PTSD can be a thing of the past.

ASK YOURSELF

Do I cry or get angry easily in relationships?

When in conflict, do I lose the ability to think and communicate effectively?

When I'm triggered, do I disassociate or go into a trance?

Do I yell, argue, defend, pout, and runaway, or use other childlike behaviors to deal with conflict?

What and/or who triggers me into a regressive state?

Why do *these* people and situations trigger me?

What can I do *immediately,* to help me get out of a triggered state?

CONCEPT 7

Loyalty to the Perpetrator

Loyalty to the Perpetrator

I f we have been abused, neglected, or had an inconsistent unpredictable childhood, we will be holding a belief in our memory that there is something wrong with us; that we are bad and also make bad things happen. These are not logical thoughts; they are deeply rooted beliefs we hold about ourselves. Recall *Concept 4: Locus of Control* where, as children, we believed we made *everything* happen.

As an adult we will have a tendency to treat ourselves the same way as our parents treated us. If we were neglected and/or abandoned we will neglect ourselves, abandoning our needs over and over. If there was physical abuse, we find that we harm ourselves through addictions, eating disorders or even types of self-mutilation such as cutting, burning or scratching ourselves. Perhaps our parents spoke to us in disparaging and critical ways, then we may find our inner dialogue is filled with calling ourselves stupid and worthless, or we may find ourselves repeating whatever dismissive or cruel words our caregivers used.

Another way of looking at *Loyalty to the Perpetrator* as children, if we were noticed when we excelled at sports or academia we might, as adults, be driven to perfection in many areas even if it is hurting us or our family. Perhaps we were called a failure or told we would never amount to much; in this case, we may find ourselves sabotaging any attempt at success as an adult by telling ourselves we can't do it. An example of how I experienced this in my own life was my mother who frequently said that I was the "cute one" while my sister was the "smart one." There was no question that my sister would go off to college after she graduated while I would never consider that as an option for myself. Instead I was cute enough to get a guy to marry me at the young age of 18-years-old. After many years of trials and tribulation I challenged my own *Loyalty to the Perpetrator* by saying, "I'm cute AND smart…and anything else I want to be!" "I am defining myself from now on!" As a result of this new way of looking at myself, I ended up attending college and I was thrilled to realize just how intelligent I really am!

Yet another example of *Loyalty to the Perpetrator* that I have seen many times is a person who was sexually abused as a child and now has some kind of sexual acting out dysfunction. Sexual abuse doesn't always involve physical contact. Sexual abuse and/or confusion can also result from witnessing or hearing a parent's promiscuous behavior, nudity of an opposite sex parent, affairs of one or the other parent, incest of a sibling, making a child a "partner" when there is discord between the parents, inappropriate sexual remarks regarding a child or teen's body, and/or exposure to pornography. Sexual acting out as an adult can be promiscuity, anonymous sex, creating unsafe sexual situations, overuse of pornography, excessive masturbation – even to the point of physically harming our body, or perhaps working in the sex industry as a prostitute or dancer.

Sexual anorexia (the shutting down of one's sexual desire) although hidden, is another form of sexual self-abuse. The saying "First at the hands of others and then at our own", certainly has meaning here.

Eating disorders can also be an example of *Loyalty to the Perpetrator*. Violating our body by withholding food or manipulating what goes in/out and when, is often a reenactment of having our body violated as a child. Another result could be overeating; this acts as both a personal violation and also as an attempt to build a protective barrier of weight to keep others away.

ASK YOURSELF

How do I define myself?

Is this really how I see myself or is it a repeat of what my caregivers told me?

What are the words and dialogue I have with myself when I'm sad, lonely, angry or afraid?

What do I say to myself when I make a mistake or struggle with an issue?

Has someone hurt me as a child and I now am hurting myself in a similar way?

Do I have thoughts, feelings and behaviors that reflect some painful dynamics of my childhood?

CONCEPT 8

Reenactment

Reenactment

The brain is a survival organ and it now holds in-memory everything you need to know to survive. You are alive and the hardwiring of your brain will direct you to recreate the same dynamics that were present while it was wiring. It knows what you can and have survived until now and anything new or different poses as a threat to that survival. This is why they say, "Bad habits are hard to break". The truth is your brain doesn't want you to change, even if it's what you want more than anything!

You will find yourself drawn to the same kind of people that mom and dad were. All the same conflicted feelings will be present as well. If we examine our lives closely we will discover that the people that you are in most conflict with *re-mind* you of your mom, dad, siblings and other people from your childhood who you struggled with.

In intimate relationships, it is less about attraction and more about recognition. We are energetically pulled toward people with whom we see parts of ourselves. Remember, from my story, the partners I chose were men who were drug-addicted like my mother was. They didn't necessarily need to be drug addicted either; I also found myself taking up the company of men who were in some way unavailable, which was exactly how the drug addiction affected my mom. Not only was she unavailable, she was inconsistent, unreliable and selfish, as were the people in my intimate relationships. As a child I was a victim because I couldn't leave or create healthy boundaries. Later, in my re-enacted relationships, I continued to see myself as a victim and saw the drug addict/alcoholic person in my life as my perpetrator. I also saw myself as the rescuer who was going to help these men live a happier and healthier life. The missing part to that formula was these men did not want to be rescued by me and resented my every attempt.

Interestingly, I also was attracted to men who had the positive characteristics of my parents. They were charming and talented musicians like my father and were intelligent artists, just as my mother was. Today, I slow down when I meet someone I might consider having an intimate relationship with. I ask a lot of questions and look for the similarities and the differences in behaviors and characteristics with regard to those of my original attachment figures.

The reenactment will often show up in our career choices as well. My example was choosing nursing as a profession. I was my mother's rescuer in childhood and as an adult, surrounded myself with the sick. I was hardwired to tend to their every need and was excellent at this job, even though it was not what I wanted to be doing with my life's work. Before my rewiring, I reenacted the rescuer role in both my job and my intimate relationships. Today, I'm happy to say that my work is that which I have a strong passion for and I am greatly rewarded in many ways for my efforts.

ASK YOURSELF

What are the similarities between my childhood and my adult life?

What are the harmful and helpful characteristics of my original attachment figures?

Do my current attachment figures have some of those same characteristics?

Do I feel the same way deep down as I did when I was young?

Do I see myself as a victim, my partner as a perpetrator?

Who plays the role of the rescuer in my life?

How about my career choice, is that as a reenacting what I learned as a child?

Am I passionate about my work or is it something I just happen to be good at?

CONCEPT 9

Hiding Feelings

Hiding Feelings

As children we are often taught not to feel and/or that our feelings are unimportant and don't matter. Often if we expressed fear, we might have been told we were silly, not to be a "scaredy cat," or that there was nothing to be afraid of. Perhaps we were afraid of the dark and just needed some encouragement from our parental figure.

It makes sense to have the feelings of fear in these and many other situations, especially as small children who are completely dependent on our parents and vulnerable. Yet if we are scolded and made to feel we are bad and/or wrong for having and expressing that feeling of fear, we will learn to push it down and deny it. Remember, we must attach to our caregivers and, if necessary, dismiss our feelings in order to receive approval. We will do that in order to improve our chances to attach. Similarly, if we cried, we might have been ridiculed and called a "cry baby". However, our little human body knows it's natural to grieve losses. I remember being told, "Stop that crying or I'll give you something to cry about!" I quickly learned to stifle my feelings of pain and sadness. An expression of anger as a child was often met with an even angrier response from our parents and we were likely to be threatened with physical pain or being sent away to be alone with our feelings. Sadly, even the expression of joy could be met with being told to settle down and be quiet. We concluded that it was better to not have feelings at all.

Societal and social pressures add to the confusion of feelings. Girls are often taught that it is not OK to be angry but that it is acceptable to be sad. Boys, on the other hand, are taught to be tough, not to feel scared or sad – "big boys don't cry," – but that anger is appropriate for them. It's no wonder we try to hide any expression of feeling.

I often ask my clients how they are *feeling*, to which a common response is, "I don't know" and I believe them. Or they may respond, "I feel fine" which isn't a feeling at all. This is similar to answering, "I feel depressed" which also isn't a feeling but a shutting down and numbing out of *feeling*. It is no wonder we have no idea how we are *actually* feeling with all of the negative messages we have received. Now we are embedded in a world in which we use drugs, alcohol, work, exercise, Facebook, eating, television, Internet browsing, sex, shopping, etc.; allowing an even more convenient escape from our feelings.

Recall from *Concept 1: Understanding Your Brain and Body* that our feelings are meant to be expressed and discharged from the human body. Our feelings are driven by powerful neurological activity and hormones; when that energy is suppressed and held in the body it can create a multitude of bodily harm such as stomach ulcers, anxiety issues, high blood pressure, Fibromyalgia (among other autoimmune disorders) TMJ, migraines, and cancers to name a few. Therefore another place to escape our emotional feelings could be to the hospital with somatic symptoms.

ASK YOURSELF

Do I dismiss or diminish my feelings?

Would I know and/or admit my feelings, if I were to be asked?

Do I let myself cry?

Am I careful not to show my emotions?

What were the messages I received about expressing my feelings when I was a child?

Do I find relief from feelings by using people, places and things to distract me?

Do I now understand that my feelings are the energy moving in my body and it requires discharge?

Do I think I may have physical symptoms due to repressed emotions?

CONCEPT 10

Addictions

Addictions

When we are traumatized, we will eventually find ways that work best for us to shut down our feelings. Maybe we learned these ways from watching our parents and how they did or did not express their feelings. If we saw an angry father pick up a drink or a sad mother being "busy-busy-busy", we will likely adopt some of those behaviors ourselves. Perhaps it wasn't safe to express feelings in your childhood home.

Often in these homes, the parents are the only ones who have the right to express feelings. As we repeatedly go to certain behaviors to diminish our feelings, especially the ones that work really well, we become more and more dependent on them. Addiction is defined as wanting to stop but being unable to, regardless of the consequences. Even though the behavior has negative results in our life and in the lives of those around us that we care about, we are somehow compelled and driven to continue the behavior despite all the painful consequences. Over time this behavior becomes an obsessive and compulsive disorder. Because of our hard wiring and beyond all logic and reasoning, we find that we are quickly overcome with thoughts of escaping these situations through our favorite method.

Addictions are very serious and can often have life threatening consequences. Our bodies can become dependent on certain chemicals and withdrawing can be painful and dangerous. We can also become dependent on our own mood states, as well. Please seek the advice of a health care professional before stopping a substance addiction, as a medically supervised detox may be necessary for your safety. If you think you have developed a physical or psychological addiction, it must be addressed so that you can really be available for this re-wiring program. Please seek help and support from an addictions specialist, a 12-step support group or an addiction recovery program. Remember: it is *truly an addiction* when even though we want to stop the behavior, and regardless of the negative consequences, we are compelled to do it anyway!

ASK YOURSELF

Is there some substance or behavior that I use over and over again which is causing negative consequences for those in my life and myself?

Did my caretakers suffer from any addictions?

Am I willing to admit that one can become addicted to people and behaviors, as well as to drugs and/or alcohol?

Do I find myself saying, "I shouldn't do this," yet it seems impossible to stop?

Am I deceiving myself when I think that "I'll do it just this one more time and *then* I'll stop or cut down?"

CONCEPT 11

The Problem is not the *Real* Problem

The Problem is not the *Real* Problem

Let's say a client comes in to see me for an appointment and they state that they have a problem with drinking or some type of eating disorder, or perhaps they are fighting with their partner; these are just a few of the presenting problems that clients might express to me for why they are seeking some help. Almost always, I can quickly assess that many of those stated "problems" are really the "solutions" to deeper, unacknowledged issues. Take the drinking client, for instance. Drinking could be the client's solution to the problem of not being able to express their feelings due to the negative consequences they experienced as a child when they did demonstrate their feelings. The client may have begun drinking at an early age thereby missing important brain developmental stages that offered healthy coping strategies for living.

Perhaps today they notice they are incapable of negotiating situations in an effective manner which causes them low self-esteem, embarrassment and distress. If they continue to drink in an uncontrollable manner, they don't have to *feel* and they're able to numb out. They are also likely to create so many consequences around excessive drinking that everyone (including themselves) are distracted from the real problem – which could be the fact that their childhood was confusing and unpredictable, and they did not have a secure healthy attachment.

This could also be the *real* problem of the person who has an eating disorder. The eating disorder may be a symptom of the real problem, which might be that someone violated their body or somehow controlled them in an unhealthy way. Take the situation of the couple who states their problem is fighting constantly; perhaps the fighting and the conflicted relationship could be the *solution* to the real problem which is the fear of attachment because as a child, attachment hurt.

It is likely we don't understand that we are using the Internet, TV, shopping, gambling, sex, drugs, food, alcohol, codependency, etc. in order *not* to have to deal with the complexity of our *real* problem which often is; growing up was difficult, there was so much pain and confusion happening all around. We didn't really know how to deal with all of that and still don't, so our solution becomes avoidance and distractions to tune out from our lives. These distractions eventually create destructive issues of their own and then the real problem gets buried even deeper.

ASK YOURSELF

What do I believe my problems are?

Is it possible that there is a deeper issue beneath the problem I am currently experiencing?

Could it be that the conflict I am dealing with is a symptom of something else?

Is my problem only acting as my solution, when it's actually just an effective distraction from a deeper problem?

CONCEPT 12

Feel Your Feelings

Feel Your Feelings

I often talk about this Concept when I give lectures on relapse prevention at substance abuse treatment facilities. There is a handout that is used by many of these facilities that shows circles representing faces wearing several different expressions. It is meant to help the clients get in touch with their feelings and identify what emotion they might be feeling. I try to keep things much simpler by teaching that there are only four *primary* feelings and they are anger, fear, sadness and joy/peace. I'll contradict myself here and say there is one more emotion, which is love. I will address that emotion in another book I am writing about healthy sexuality. Someone might ask, "What about *jealousy?*" My response is that all other so-called feelings are actually a combination of a couple of primary feelings. So let's look at jealousy. This is a combination of anger and fear. What about shame or guilt? These begin as thoughts such as, "I am bad, wrong or what I did was bad or wrong", and those thoughts trigger the emotions of sadness and/or fear.

Now, you may have noticed that sometimes I use the word feeling and at other times use the word emotion. Are they the same thing? Yes...*and* No! I'll explain. When I use the word emotion I am referring to *energy-in-motion*. We all learned in our biology class in high school that everything is composed of energy; some things vibrate at a high frequency and others at a much slower frequency. Isn't it correct that if we were able to look through a high-power microscope at literally anything, we would see the molecules of that energy moving?

Think about the energy of the human body. Our brain is full of electrical energy, as is our heart. We can measure this energy through the use of medical instruments such as an EEG or EKG. Our heart and brain are not the only parts of our body filled with energy. Energy exists throughout our entire body. I refer to this energy movement as *e-motion*. So what about feelings? I teach people to *feel* the movement of that energy, especially when triggered. Because, as I stated in *Concept 9: Hiding Feelings*, we have become numb to our feelings so often we are unaware that we are in a triggered state. When we are triggered our heart is likely to beat faster; we might feel a strange sensation in our stomach, our respirations could increase or we might hold our breath. If we are out of touch with our bodies and feelings, then we are also unaware when we are triggered! We are then likely to deal with situations from a regressive state using childlike strategies. The results will be messy at best and disastrous at worst.

What we really mean by Concept 12, is to pay attention and actually *feel* the sensation of nerve and hormonal activity in your body. Our feelings are our information system and your body is telling you that something is going on in the environment that you need to pay attention to and/or negotiate. Refer back to *Concept 1: Understanding Your Brain and Body* to gain a deeper understanding. The ability to feel this movement in your body will assist you in determining what the action will be to discharge this energy (emotion) from the body. This decision needs to be a logical one such as exercise (fight or flight hormones) or crying to discharge hormones and toxins from the body. We can discharge a lot of energy though our speech, too! People often report how much better they feel after they have talked things through with someone.

ASK YOURSELF

What is the difference between feelings and emotions?

What does my body *feel* like when I'm angry, sad, or afraid?

How about when I'm joyful and/or at peace?

Can I detect stress hormones vs. "feel good" ones?

Can I tell when I'm feeling triggered?

What are some healthy ways that I can discharge energy from my body?

CONCEPT 13

Is it a Feeling or a Thought?

Is it a Feeling or a Thought?

Our language has become quite confusing and perhaps just a little manipulative. We often hear people say things like, "I feel it's time to go" or, "I feel that was an unfair statement." Yet, we intellectually know it's time to go is not a feeling, but a thought. The same is true for saying, That's an unfair statement which is also not a feeling, but a thought or opinion. When we are trying to communicate with someone using this kind of language it is ineffective and usually ends in an argument with an unsatisfactory outcome. We confuse others (and often ourselves) about what we are actually thinking and how we truly feel about what is going on. When we use the word *feeling* constantly in our communication and especially in a conflicted situation, it has a manipulative quality to it... After all one can't argue with one's feelings, right?

Sometimes we don't know what we are feeling and/or are reluctant to express our thoughts. Conflict often triggers us into a childlike state and our memory tells us that it's not OK to speak about what we are thinking or feeling because "It wouldn't matter anyway!"– at least that's the message we received. We are subconsciously recalling the fear and sadness we experienced as a child, when we would try tell our caregivers about our feelings.

Almost every couple I see in therapy is speaking in this confusing way, mixing up feelings and thoughts, yet reporting that communication is one of their biggest issues. How can we hope to have intelligent, mature conversations using this language? This confusing language also supports *not* feeling, if *every* thought is a feeling.

It's important to know the difference between thoughts and feelings. We must learn to communicate effectively and respectfully about our thoughts, feelings and desires to others. I use the word *desires* here, because as adults the days of getting someone outside of us to fulfill our needs are over.

The unrealistic expectation of getting *needs* met in an adult relationship fosters co-dependency. As adults it's important to be able to fulfill our needs ourselves. It is equally important to be able to ask others to consider what we want and desire in the relationship. I think using the word *need* can be manipulative. Consider the statement "I need you to respect me." The truth is that respect is not a need and it's really more likely that the person making the statement wants the other person to respect them. Using the word need implies "necessary for survival" and again, as adults we must be able to take care of basic needs ourselves.

I offer the following 5-part communication formula as one that is clear, respectful and intelligent.

Let's use this example: Mary is a stay at home mom. Her husband Joe goes to work daily at his job as a contractor and her daily job is to manage the home and children. Both jobs bring value to their family and are equally stressful and demanding. Mary had a particularly difficult day when the stove stopped working and both children came down with the flu, thereby staying home from school. She couldn't get a hold of Joe all day and was eager for him to come home so she could ask him about replacing the stove, managing dinner and telling him about one of the children's worsening condition. She wanted his advice and support. When he walked in the door she said, "Joe, I want to tell you about a few things and…" but before she could finish her sentence Joe held up his hand and said, "Not now, I need to sit down, look at the paper and relax." He walked out of the room and Mary became very angry and hurt!

This is a situation where things could have gone wrong quickly! But, because Mary has been taught the 5-part communication formula and is using The 20 Concepts she realized that she was triggered and that her feelings were intense. Remembering that this means the activity is directed away from the thinking part of the brain and is concentrated in the emotional part of the brain. She takes a deep breath and relaxes her shoulders. Since deep breathing and relaxing are counterintuitive to danger, this small action signals her brain that there is no life-threatening situation happening. The body informs the brain, as well as the brain informing the body. As activity increases in the thinking part of the brain, Mary thinks about the way her father dismissed her as a teen when she would try to talk to him about things that mattered to her; then she says to herself, "That was then and this is now" and follows that with "Joe is not my father and I am not a child." She continues to stay active in her thinking part of the brain where language and formulas are also centered. She walks back into the room and uses the 5-part communication formula:

The 5-Part Communication Formula

1) This is what I saw (or heard)
This is an honest report of what happened, what Mary saw and heard when Joe came in.

Mary said, "When you got home from work earlier, I began to tell you something important and I saw you hold your hand up and say "Not now!" Then you walked out of the room."

2) This is what I think (or thought.)
This is a self-revealing account of your opinions regarding what happened.

Mary said, "I thought it was dismissive and a rude interruption. I thought that my feelings and this difficult situation didn't matter to you. I thought it was unfair and selfish because of all the times I have listened to you, even if I was tired. I thought...you don't really care about me."

3) This is how I feel (or felt)

Be sure you are using the 4 feelings (anger, sad, fear or joy)

Mary said, "I felt really angry and sad, too!"

4) This is what I want (not need).

Be specific in stating it's your desire and that's all!

Mary said, "I want you to take a few minutes when you get home and talk with me. I want you to listen and care about the things that I struggle with, like I do for you. I want you to speak kindly and show me respect. I want to matter to you and for you to show me you care about me."

5) Are you willing?

This question is designed to get a yes or no answer...sometimes someone will say that they will try or perhaps they may want to negotiate. Perhaps in this case Joe asks for 10 minutes or so to wind down before he hears about the problems that await him at home. That's not unreasonable.

Mary said "Are you willing to do this with me?"

The point is that we communicate this way not to influence a particular outcome, but because what we think, how we feel and what we want matters and it's important enough to say it out loud! It also opens up a dialogue instead of holding onto anger and creating distance in the relationship.

This communication formula is also a very effective journaling exercise when we are indecisive about how to deal with a situation. Writing down what is happening now, what we are thinking about it, what we really want and then asking ourselves if we are willing to do our part to have what's important to us?

ASK YOURSELF

Am I communicating honestly?

Do I frequently substitute the word feeling when I really want to express a thought or opinion?

Am I afraid to express my thoughts and opinions?

In my childhood did my thoughts and opinions seem to matter?

Am I clear to others what I actually want in any given situation?

Do I believe my wants are important?

Does someone have to guess what I want?

Am I willing to write down this formula *before* I have a conversation so that I am clear about what I think, feel and want?

Can I begin to see how using The 20 Concepts, offer a more intelligent and effective way to negotiate life's situations?

CONCEPT 14

Thinking/Feeling/
Behavior Loop

Thinking/Feeling/
Behavior Loop

At last, my favorite concept! I love them all and they all have tremendous power, yet the *Thinking/Feeling/Behavior Loop* is the one that absolutely gets me the most excited! I am so passionate about this concept because it is truly one of the strongest on re-wiring!

Nerve and hormonal activation in the brain and body not only occur by outside triggers, as described in *Concept 6: Triggers to Regression*, but can, and often does, occur as a result of our own thoughts. We all have had some frightening thoughts about what's in store for us, what some people are likely to be thinking about us, and/or why someone did what they did. These negative thoughts are very powerful and our imagination (story-telling) will activate stress hormones; and as a result, our behavior will be that of a stressed being. Remember, the subconscious survival brain doesn't compute time, nor does it know the difference between what is real and what's imagined.

"Time" is a formula created through thought and words. It certainly is true that the sun rises and sets and that the weather changes with the movement of the globe, but the word time and the system and tools we call a calendar and clock are creations. They first existed as a thought. More about *thoughts* becoming *things*, a little later.

Now we look at what's real versus what's imagined. We can and do activate neurological/hormonal responses through our thinking and imagining. This is why hypnotherapy is such an incredibly successful treatment for compulsive behaviors as well as physical ailments. I always begin a hypnotherapy session by asking clients to relax and breathe slowly. I tell them to imagine their lungs slowly filling with air and releasing that air. I instruct them to imagine their heart rate slowing down and to feel their face and body relaxing. I am observing the client carefully during these instructions and I can see their face relax and notice their respirations slow down.

As the client starts to imagine what I've described, his or her body responds accordingly. The client's conscious brain has little activity and their subconscious is regulating breath, heart rate and muscle tone. I am instructing the client throughout the session to imagine their desired outcome. When the client leaves the session they are calm and centered. They now have in their memory (subconscious) an experience of the outcome they desired. Often clients call me back reporting that things have changed and that they are no longer drawn to self-defeating behaviors. They also find themselves motivated to adopt the behaviors that they wanted to implement in their lives.

Here is another example of the time/thought phenomenon of the subconscious mind. A client came into my office and began to tell me about something that happened over 30 years ago when he was only 8 years old. His father took his dog out and shot it because my client had forgotten to give it water that morning (I know, very disturbing). As my client was thinking about that dreadful day, he began to sob. Why would my client cry 30 years after the event? He is an adult man and yet his tears are that of a child. Stimulated by his thought, the subconscious part of his brain was neurologically activated, stimulating a hormonal response and the behavior was crying. Crying releases hormones and toxins from the body. My client's *thinking* activated *feelings*, which activated a *behavior*.

I'll provide one more example of real versus imagined. A client came in for a session and told me that she thought her husband was cheating on her with her best friend. She had no proof other than he had seemed preoccupied recently and she reported that upon walking into their bedroom one evening when he was on the phone, she noticed he quickly hung up. When she asked with whom he was speaking he replied, "No one. It's not important." He then immediately changed the subject to something totally unrelated, and proceeded to tell her what the children wanted do for the upcoming family weekend. She looked at his cell phone when he left the room and saw that he had been talking to her best friend. She said she was furious! Her thinking was, "My husband is having an affair with my best friend." This created an abundance of fight or flight hormonal activity and she felt angry and afraid. Her behavior was about to become aggressive and she told me that she was planning to "get in her friend's face" as soon as she left my office. I suggested she not entirely believe the story she was telling herself (her thoughts) and instead asked her to first speak with her husband and express her thoughts and feelings. She reluctantly agreed. It turned out that her husband and her best friend were planning a surprise birthday party for her, which explained the earlier preoccupation and the suspicious phone call. The point is that our thinking (imagination) will create nerve/hormonal responses, and our behavior is a response to that activation.

The *Thinking/Feeling/Behavior Loop* can create and wreak more havoc than many real situations. I am constantly asking clients if the story they are telling themselves is based on true facts. And so many times it is not! If you had a childhood where you were betrayed and hurt, you will likely have a tendency to imagine bad things will happen. After all, it's what you know. Unfortunately, that kind of thinking keeps you in a state of fear, anger, and pain.

I instruct clients when they are out of my office to be *mindful* of their thoughts and if they are activating stress. I ask them to ask themselves if their thoughts are true and based on fact. If they are not, I ask them to investigate and ask questions or to simply replace the thought with "I'm not sure if this is true". I also ask them to remember *Concept 4: Locus of Control,* which states that "All I can control in life is my thinking, my feelings and my behavior." Remembering this will immediately have a calming effect as the thought changes from the stress hormone-activating one of "I have to control someone and I can't" to "I can only control my thoughts, feelings, and behaviors." This helps the body to close the receptors for stress hormones and we begin to feel better.

Thoughts that are peaceful and joyful will activate positive hormonal responses and our behavior will reflect that! Think of a time you were appreciated, when someone did something kind for you or told you how much he or she admired you... How do you feel? How about thinking of a time when something really funny happened... Are you smiling? There is no question that thinking creates feelings and feelings motivate behavior.

There is so much power in the thinking/creative part of the brain. Are we remembering to use it to create our reality? Today this is one of the areas that I am extra attentive to. If I catch myself having a negative thought, I immediately redirect my thought to a better, healthier one and my body responds accordingly. Today I have no fear other than a situation that could truly endanger my life or wellbeing. If I'm angry, my mind is telling me that a boundary has been crossed or a real injustice has been done.

Anger should motivate us to take an action for equality, never revenge. Our pain and sadness always has to do with some kind of loss. Remember, our feelings exist to inform us that something is happening that we need to pay attention to and they help us navigate or negotiate the situation. When stress hormones are not managed and discharged from the body; that energy breaks down the internal organs and illness can follow. The old quote, "The body bears the burden" certainly applies here. While an abundance of stress hormones in the body is harmful to us, high levels of "feel good" hormones cause the body to function at an optimum level.

ASK YOURSELF

Since I am thinking most of the time when I'm awake, what kind of thoughts am I having?

What are the stories I tell myself about the world and the people in it?

Do I think I am a victim and someone else a perpetrator?

Do I think someone else is a victim who I should rescue?

Do I find my thoughts are of lack and deprivation, and my feelings are fear or anger?

How do I feel when I think negatively compared to how I feel when I have thoughts of love, peace, and joy?

When I think of funny situations do I find myself smiling?

Will I accept that I can create my reality based on my thoughts, feelings and behavior?

CONCEPT 15

Anchors to Triggers

Anchors to Triggers

An anchor is something that stops you in your tracks! Think of a boat heading towards an iceberg; throwing out an anchor will stop that boat from reaching its doom. When triggered in PTSD, we are heading into a regressive state and we now understand that this is a very childlike state. We can't have adult, productive lives using childlike strategies anymore. We must create anchors to stop the regression when we are triggered. The very first step is to *feel* the sensations in your body so you begin to know and understand when you are being triggered. The first anchor is to take a deep breath and drop your shoulders; the body informs the brain as well as the brain informing the body. This behavior sends a signal to the brain that the crisis is over.

As stress receptors in the brain begin to close you will increase activity in the thinking part of the brain and you can ask yourself how to get away (get a little space) from the trigger. Sometimes, just a few minutes away from the situation will keep us out of a regressive state. Asking to have a minute to use the bathroom works well. If you are in a car or area in which you cannot get away you can say, "I'm triggered and prefer not to speak about this for now."

Anchors are breathing, relaxing the body, and if possible, walking away for a while. Think about not only what happened that triggered you but also how you can use the 5-part-communication in the situation. Remember we use the communication formula not to "get what we want," but because it keeps us connected to our intellect instead of spewing words based on re-acting – and we have a right to tell the truth about how we see any situation and how we would like it to be. Again, our thoughts, feelings and desires are valid enough to speak out loud! When done so using the 5-part-communication, our words have a much better chance of being heard and suddenly we are able to communicate while maintaining our integrity.

This thinking and formulating language keeps the cerebral cortex active. The more you use anchors when triggered the more you stay in a mature, adult state. The goal is to create rapid firing neuropathways from our emotional survival brain to our logical thinking brain where language and formulas exist. A most effective formula now in memory, is The 20 Concepts.

ASK YOURSELF

Am I in touch with my feelings, so that I recognize when I'm triggered?

Once I realize that I am being triggered, what are my anchors?

Am I willing to continuously use them until they become hardwired in my brain?

Will I speak intelligently and respectfully with anyone about my thoughts, feelings and desires?

CONCEPT 16

Modulation

Modulation

This concept may seem simple but it is one of the most significant concepts to the re-wiring process. All the previous concepts have been teaching you how to accomplish this one. To modulate means to increase or decrease something at will, which is very different from shutting down our feelings. In this case, we want to learn to modulate our feelings, reactions, thoughts, and behaviors. This is the concept that will instruct us how to master our own human organism! When we become skilled at this, our whole life changes in ways we can only imagine. A helpful way to understand modulation is to think of a dial on an oven, for instance. When we turn it one direction the oven gets hotter, turn it the other and the temperature decreases. We have learned that we are more able to think maturely and take care of our bodies when we decrease stress; we have also learned that high levels of stress hormones, harms our physical body. Remember *Concept 14: Thinking /Feeling/Behavior Loop*? Our thoughts will influence our body and our behavior will reflect how we feel.

Here is an example: I was working with a client who would get an angry look on his face every time I would mention his mother. I asked him how he felt when I brought up his mom. He said, "Angry. She was a selfish woman." Knowing the history of this client's relationship with his mother in childhood, I understood how he had come to think of her this way. His feelings of anger were appropriate! Yet, some of these thoughts and feelings were interfering with his ability to perceive women in any way other than as selfish, which in turn impeded his ability to form healthy intimate relationships with them. We explored his mother's childhood, which was riddled with poverty and neglect. At age 17 she married a partner who was often emotionally and physically absent. She gave birth to a special needs baby a year later and within two years she had a second baby, a healthy boy. She was 21 years old when her husband decided to leave the country for three years. As I began to express compassion and empathy for her dire situation, he modulated his anger and integrated some sadness, realizing that his mom went through devastating times. He recently reached out to his mother, and took her to lunch and they talked about the past with a greater acceptance and understanding. He is committed to using the concept of modulation whenever he feels strongly about something because he has gained the knowledge that modulation allows for a shift in thought. That shift in thought can create an understanding that results in a behavior that is more peaceful and accepting. In one of our subsequent sessions he cried about all the time that was wasted feeling angry, as well as how poorly he treated his mom when they *were* around each other. He was able to again modulate his feelings of sadness with the intelligent thought, "I will make up for it now by showing her my love and spending more time with her!"

As we mindfully decrease stress hormones through modulation, we increase feel-good hormones like serotonin, endorphins, and oxytocin. When we are abundant in these hormones we remain calm, focused, and aware of all that life has to offer; and we desire to be connected to others in a kind and loving way, which is what happened when my client modulated his anger regarding his thoughts of his mother.

Modulation can be used as a form of meditation, although it can be accomplished in a matter of moments by taking a couple of slow, deep breaths as in *Concept 15: Anchors to Triggers*. In addition to meditation, this breathing is also used in yoga, Tai Chi and Qi Gong. It is also a known stress and anxiety reducer because of its therapeutic calming effect. There is a reason that people who meditate are healthier in their bodies and seem less worried and more productive. Again, less activity in the survival brain increases activity in the conscious brain; where our intelligence and creativity is located.

Have you heard the saying "Thoughts Become Things?" Who knows where this saying first originated? I've seen it mentioned in the Bible, by Gandhi, and by Einstein. It has been repeatedly referenced by philosophers and inventors over hundreds of years.

The laptop I am writing on was first someone's creative thought, so was the iPhone I carry around continuously. Actually, as I look around this room, everything was first someone's thought. Take a moment now and look around you. Is there anything that wasn't originated by someone's thought? The power of thought! Recall the client I just wrote about; recall his thoughts about his mother and how changing the way he thought about her, made him feel differently about her. His behavior changed and he reached out to spend time with her. Their relationship now reflects his new thoughts about her. Through modulation we truly do master our brain so that we can create a reality that is filled with joy, peace and abundance. This doesn't mean we won't still have struggles and some bitter moments; this concept and all the others are tools that will help us improve our lives and enjoy the sweet moments more; but also it's aimed at helping us get through the bitter ones perhaps a little quicker, and a little easier. Getting back to place of joy and peace with even more integrity and self-confidence that we can make it through anything is our ultimate goal.

ASK YOURSELF

Am I ready to become a master of my own human mind and body?

Will I choose to decrease stress and increase peacefulness?

Does my body feel better when it's relaxed and I'm joyful?

What does my body feel like when I'm filled with stress?

Will I learn to modulate my reactions to what once triggered me?

When I am less stressed do I notice that I think more positively?

What are some past or current situations where if I had modulated my feelings; things could be more peaceful?

What are the creative thoughts I have for my present?

What would I like my future to look like?

Am I willing to practice modulation of my thoughts, feelings and behaviors daily, in order to change my life for the better?

CONCEPT 17

Desensitization

Desensitization

Through the use of The 20 Concepts, we become less and less "sensitive" to other people and situations. We are not so easily triggered by people, places or things that activate the survival part of our brain. Through the understanding and practicing of all the previous concepts, we no longer need to insist that others "take care of us" by changing their behaviors. We allow people to be themselves. Our reactions are often coming from old wiring... To *re-act* is to "act as one has before." Instead, we think about what might be causing people to behave the way they do. We can respond using a more intelligent part of our brain; the part that we want significantly involved in determining our executive functioning and behavior.

Of course, desensitization never suggests that we tolerate any form of abuse or neglect. We can use the communication formula learned in *Concept 13: Is it a Feeling or a Thought* to address those situations. We establish healthy boundaries and a firm respect for ourselves. Sometimes it's necessary to walk away and perhaps stay away. Through this work we become increasingly clear about what's appropriate for our best self-care.

Lastly, this concept simply means that although a situation may be triggering, we can choose to tolerate it, modulate our thoughts and feelings and negotiate it. Through exposure to challenging situations we can use desensitization rather than re-act and run away. By the time we are actively using this concept we will have already developed a deep understanding of what kinds of situations are safe and worthwhile to negotiate and which are more appropriate to remove ourselves from.

ASK YOURSELF

Can I let people be who and how they are?

Am I willing to modulate so that I can think clearly and be better able to make a decision whether I should desensitize or walk away?

Will I challenge myself to think about reactions (to act as I did before) versus responses (using the concepts in the present) to act intelligently?

What are the situations in which desensitization could benefit me?

CONCEPT 18

Integration

Integration

I often say integration is the backbone for The 20 Concepts and for living in general. Using this concept keeps us out of "either/or", "us/them", and "black/white" thinking. Integration means "bringing together" and brings a mature focus to life. Let's look at the blending together of opposites in the following example: A woman came to see me claiming that her partner was emotionally abusive. The only two options she saw were to *either* leave him *or* put up with the abuse. This is clearly a case of black and white thinking. Black and white thinking is also referred to as "child-like" thinking due to the fact that children are not capable of understanding complex situations logically.

As an adult, this woman could use integration here, by blending several options to come to a final decision. One option would be using the 5-part communication formula. She could state her thoughts and feelings about what was happening and ask for what she wanted such as kindness and respect. Another option for her could be to ask her partner to attend couples counseling or perhaps even ask for a trial separation to give each person an opportunity to see how they each felt being apart. None of these options are the either/or options she came in with. Ultimately this couple may decide to divorce, but the decision would be a thoughtful one, with the integration of other possibilities first.

Another way of using integration is when we examine our childhood and the negative characteristics of our parents. When we practice integration we also acknowledge that they had *positive* characteristics that we can embrace as a part of ourselves. Remember in my life story, my mother was a prescription drug addict, but she was also very intelligent and creative artistically. I have integrated the truth that she contributed to my intelligence as well as my creativity and artistic nature.

My codependent father was a great musician and livened up any room he entered; I also have an outstanding appreciation for music and love to engage in playfulness in life. As I got out of black and white thinking I was able to care about my parents and not see them as entirely evil. Integration also helped me acknowledge the qualities that I have and that fostered self-love and respect. So often we find ourselves being critical of the mistakes we make and spend very little time actually acknowledging that we are "pretty darn good" people.

In regards to my childhood I have used the concept of integration to invite my past into my present. Trying to forget (you won't) or get over your past (you can't because of the brain's memory) is a waste of time and effort. It is so much healthier to embrace the past as an important part of yourself and find meaning in integrating it. For me, while it is true that I was my mother's rescuer as a child, I developed an amazing capacity to support and assist those who are suffering. Can you see how using the this concept has helped me to acknowledge my talents in a healthy way?

When there is anger in our bodies, there is also sadness and loss. Think about a situation in which you believed someone did something unfair or betrayed you in some way. Do you sense the anger? Now think about what might have been lost in that situation; was it loss of respect; loss of consideration for your feelings, your time, your hopes? Perhaps it was the loss of the relationship. Allow yourself to feel that sadness along with the anger. Anger and pain are the opposite sides of the same coin of emotion. We never have one without the other and acknowledging that helps us to become integrated and behave more appropriately.

It is the same idea with thinking and feeling. Subconscious memory and its associated feelings become integrated with the conscious, intellectual part of our brain; this enables us to make choices that are mature and responsible.

And finally, we integrate our fragmented selves into a whole. We don't neglect our survival needs (child) instead we hold the little self delicately, addressing needs for care and guidance while providing play and learning. We also embrace our sexual and adventurous self (adolescent or teenager) while providing healthy and safe guidelines. We respect our wisdom and maturity (adult) acting with intelligence, kindness, wisdom and grace. We ultimately become the *best parent* to ourselves and we are proud of who we are.

ASK YOURSELF

Do I allow myself to feel my anger *and* my sadness, acknowledging that when one is present so is the other?

Am I avoiding or rejecting a time in my life, or a part of myself?

Am I using mindfulness to be aware of my thoughts, as well as my feelings?

Do I notice myself becoming more aware of when I *feel* triggered and integrating what I've learned?

Do I use black and white thinking, and either/or options?

Am I willing to integrate my subconscious memory and feelings into my conscious – thinking mind so I can understand myself better?

If I get to know and integrate *all* parts of myself, can I imagine how I will live differently?

CONCEPT 19

Tolerate the Discomfort

Tolerate the Discomfort

Understanding the brain as a "survival" organ and realizing that change presents as a "threat" is paramount! We are starting to come full circle with the concepts and as we learned in the first concept, memory is first and foremost a system that is crucial for our survival. Memory informs us what to move towards and what to move away from. Attempting to make big changes will first activate the brain, causing a search in memory to check if this decision is something that has been encountered and survived previously. If it is not recognized, it will be processed by the brain as a survival threat and will result in the activation of stress hormones. We will *feel* the discomfort of that physiological process and perhaps stop moving forward with change. We may find ourselves saying things like, "I'm really not comfortable with this" or "that way of doing things is just not me".

As mentioned before, no one is suggesting that we do anything that is disrespectful or unhealthy: matter of fact, what we are attempting to do is begin a new way of thinking and behaving in the world that is quite the opposite! Tolerating the discomfort teaches the brain that not only can we survive the new thought and behavior, but that this actually enhances our lives. With repetition of this concept we will rewire the brain, creating a new memory. The discomfort will in fact go away once there is a new pattern, new wiring, and a new way. Therefore we only need tolerate the discomfort in the beginning. Expecting that it will be uncomfortable to make changes helps us to tolerate that temporary discomfort and keeps us moving forward with our commitment to re-wire.

ASK YOURSELF

Now that I know my brain doesn't want me to change and why, am I willing to tolerate some discomfort in order to re-wire and create new memory?

Do I understand that discomfort is a fear response to the unknown?

By doing things differently, can I see that I will desensitize to that discomfort?

Am I able to *really* grasp the power I have to "change my mind"?

Am I ready to really live, and not just survive?

CONCEPT 20

Adult Responsibility is Non-Negotiable

Adult Responsibility is Non-Negotiable

This final concept demands that we use the concepts to achieve the ability to *respond* to all of life in a *mature, adult* way, which is our ultimate goal. There is no need to negotiate it; if it is not what you desire for your life then these concepts are of no use to you. Refusing to take on this "adult responsibility" of using concepts to re-wire does not make you bad or wrong, it simply means that this is not the method you choose. Many of us can see the benefit of being able to respond to life in an intelligent and mature way rather than continuing to re-act.

Starting with the very first concept, *Understanding Your Brain and Body* and how it functions, then layering on the other concepts, gives us the ability to use intelligent, caring, and compassionate behavior in a consistent manner in all our affairs. Gone are the days of yelling, crying hysterically, dissociating and acting out. Addictions, seeing people as perpetrators and ourselves as victims, or compulsively rescuing and enabling people are in the past. Through this work we have picked up the missing pieces of our childhood development; pieces missed due to the stress of attempting to survive in an environment where there were too many challenges for our young minds to navigate. Gone are the days of being too busy trying to achieve the secure attachment we were unable to obtain as children with those who were in charge of our safety.

This concept of adult responsibility addresses basic self-care such as adequate sleep, medical/dental attention, financial wisdom, proper nutrition and exercise, setting healthy boundaries, communicating clearly, staying away from childlike behaviors, catching ourselves when using regressive thinking and/or repeating destructive patterns – and it asks us to manage our feelings. This is indeed a tall order, yet using The 20 Concepts repeatedly will make this way of being and living, second nature.

ASK YOURSELF

Will I take responsibility for my life today and going forward?

Can I accept that all my emotional and physical needs are now my responsibility?

Am I ready to use mature and adult communication to address people and negotiate situations?

Now that I understand how, will I rewire my brain so I can live an amazing life?

Is it time to create a vision of how I want my life to look?

Can I see that the concepts are the vehicle to use to achieve that vision?

Am I ready to take responsibility in evolving my own mind and therefore contributing to the evolution of the human species?

FIVE

How to Rewire

HOW TO REWIRE

It's Simple but Not Easy!

Rewiring the brain does not happen immediately, although I find that people who have begun using these tools think, feel and behave differently very quickly. In order to see long term change and *actually* rewire the brain, we must have a strong desire and be ready to commit to the process.

Just as it takes time and repetition to learn to play the piano or speak a new language, it is no different when it comes to rewiring the brain. It is said, "Neurons that fire together, wire together" meaning that the more a neuron fires in a certain direction, the deeper and more significant that pathway becomes. There is also another saying, which is "use it or lose it," and that definitely applies here. If you stop using a neurological thought process, eventually it becomes less and less available. If you stop using The 20 Concepts in your life, you will be unable to retain the memory of these tools and your thoughts, feelings, and behavior will likely return to a regressive state.

Think about this example; a person is 20 pounds over the weight they desire and they are concerned about their health. They decide to eat healthier and start exercising. After several months of this new healthy behavior, they have lost the unwanted weight and are happy with how much more their muscles are defined! They feel better about their health, body and fitness.

Now, what do you think would happen if they stopped eating healthy and decided to no longer exercise? How long do you think it would take for them to find themselves right back where they started, unhappy and unhealthy? It is exactly the same with re-wiring, use it or lose it!

The good news is when you use the concepts consistently in your life they become a habit and become the "new way" of living, as opposed to the old reactionary way. The concepts will eventually become second nature to you and old, ineffective habits will seem foreign and unhealthy.

Our goal here is to create rapid firing neuropathways that move from the survival (subconscious) emotional part of the brain to the thinking (conscious) creative part of the brain. Through repetition those pathways become deeply grooved. Whenever you *feel* stressed... Think of the concepts! Doing this again and again creates that hard wiring and after a while the pathways activate spontaneously and your life will become less stressed. You will live a more conscious, joyful and productive life. This rewiring is likely to be the most significant thing you will do in your life and it should be treated as such!

I recommend you first read and then re-read The 20 Concepts section of this book and ponder the questions asked at the end of each concept. Next, start a 20 Concepts journal and write your understanding of each question as it relates to your childhood and your adult life now. Write about your environment as a child. Think deeply about the experiences you, as a very small and innocent child, had. Allow yourself to *feel* sadness and compassion for yourself. Remember, whenever there is sadness, there is also anger present. Write in the journal about your feelings, talk about them to someone, and cry if that's what your body is telling you to do.

Write an anger letter to the person or persons who have hurt you! Don't hold back…you are not going to send this letter. It's an opportunity to express yourself and your feelings. It is likely that in our childhoods we were not allowed to express our feelings and what we had to say didn't matter. We are not attempting to blame our parents; we understand that it is probable that their childhood trapped them in a "survival life"… often using the same regressive techniques for parenting that were used by their own parents. If the person who harmed you is someone other than a parent, it's important to remember that there are no perpetrators who first were not victims themselves. Yet, that does not excuse their inappropriate behavior. Having that knowledge just makes it more understandable. The emotion of anger still needs to be discharged from the body. Writing and speaking assertively assists in that discharge; and so does any exercise that simulates fight or flight. Think about running or kickboxing. Move your body when you're feeling stressed!

Be sure to go back and answer all the questions after each concept in this book. Write the answers out in your journal and check back every month to see if your answers are different. Are you beginning to think, feel and behave differently in only a couple of months? I believe you will be surprised at how quickly this rewiring takes place. It's "keeping the wiring firing" that's crucial. Whenever you face a conflict in your life, look to The 20 Concepts to find the answer.

I offer an example below of an interaction that happened recently in my life where I used the concepts.

A good friend of mine wanted to come to San Diego for a long weekend visit and I was thrilled to have her. I began to make plans, specifically not scheduling clients and keeping my social calendar open so that I would be completely available to spend my time with her. I went to the store and bought things that I knew she would enjoy for dinners and snacks. A couple days before she was to arrive she called and said she decided to come visit a few days later than what we had planned, as she had received an invitation to a dinner party put on by a group of her friends that she thought would be fun to attend. I felt my face get hot and my heart started beating quickly; I knew I was *triggered*. I told her I needed to get off the phone and would call her back. My purpose was to get space and time away because I knew I was triggered (my body told me) and I know that my ability to communicate effectively is compromised when triggered.

Remember when emotions are activated the activity in the thinking part of the brain decreases. That is also the part of the brain that aids in communication. Leaving the situation was my first *anchor*. Once off the phone, I took a deep breath and dropped my shoulders remembering that the body sends signals to the brain, as well as the brain sending signals to the body. In this case the deep breathing and relaxing caused stress receptors to close down and enable me to think about why I was so triggered. I realized this situation "re-minded" me of my childhood and how I never knew when my mom would be the mom who was loving and available or when she would be the mean and unavailable mom.

The inconsistency and believing one thing was happening and then realizing something opposite was happening was frightening as a child. This current situation was just *similar enough* to trigger me. I told myself to stay out of the *triangle*, that I am an adult now and there is no perpetrator, and I am not a victim; today I have choices. It's also not my job to rescue or fix anyone. Next, I thought of the *Locus of Control* concept.

Again, I remind myself that I can't control anyone, but I can control myself. I then ask myself, "How do I want to behave?" "What will I do or not do?" I will check-in with my body again. By this point I have *modulated*; I am less triggered and I can take it down a few more notches if I need to, by taking a walk or talking to someone about the situation. I am not looking for advice; I already know what to do. I am taking care of myself by discharging negative energy out of my body through movement and using my voice. Eventually, I become *less sensitive* to people and their behavior whether it is immature, unhealthy or just slightly inconsiderate; such as I believed was the case in this situation. I wrote out the 5-Part Communication Formula, as I perceived the situation. I then asked myself what my thoughts, feelings and desires were and if I was clear about what I wanted? And, finally would I be willing to ask for what I want?

I called my friend back and used the 5-part formula to communicate in a mature and respectful way:

1) This is what I saw/heard
I reminded her of our original plans and told her of the things I did to prepare for her visit.

2) This is what I think.
I said I thought she didn't consider my feelings before changing her arrival date.

3) This is how I feel.
I told her I felt hurt and a little angry, too.

4) This is what I want.
I then said I wanted her to follow through with our original plans

5) Are you willing?
I asked her if she was willing to do that. She said yes and thanked me for my honesty.

Now, we will not always get what we want just because we ask for it but I am satisfied when I speak the truth about my thoughts, feeling and desires instead of carrying a resentment and then risking that it would show up in some passive-aggressive way. Of course, I was not always this way. I used to regress and use many immature behaviors to try to cope or manipulate conflicted situations, but with time, repetition, and *tolerating the discomfort* of doing things differently, my life has changed. I have become the best parent to myself and never would abandon or neglect my physical or emotional needs. This is now my *adult responsibility*. I live with *integrity* and grace. I am kind, light-hearted and playful. I am caring yet intelligent, and my *behavior* reflects that. I am a truth speaker and I have learned how to calm my *emotional brain* so that my *conscious creative brain* can guide me.

At the end of the day, we are all human and therefore do not do things perfectly - I am no different, but my *regressive* days are over. I am present and in the now. I no longer act out or hurt myself emotionally by staying *attached* to a person or situation that is disrespectful to me. I don't look to anyone to take care of my needs, as I am a capable adult. There is no *loyalty* to the past method. I'm proud of my way of being in the world. Now I can *feel my feelings* and express them appropriately. I am able to *respond* to people and situations in an *adult*, mature way. I won't *wish* or *hope* that things will be different…I must and will do something different.

I used many of The 20 Concepts in the above situation of conflict. It doesn't matter what has happened or is happening, it's how we respond that's important. Read the previous paragraph again and think about the concepts I used. I have been using this approach for years so it all happens automatically for me now. Just like the alcoholic who used to drink when stressed. Today he doesn't even think of it. I have rewired my brain so that my regressive thoughts, feelings and behaviors are a thing of the past.

At the Wisdom and Recovery Wellness Center in Portland Oregon, we have several groups that meet to talk about struggles in our lives. All supportive communication is done by practicing The 20 Concepts regarding presenting issues. These groups are comprised of advanced thinkers who continue to keep the "wiring-firing" as they know how important it is to retain this memory. Many have been coming for several years, mostly now to support the newer members. These people know that using and hearing concepts keep them hardwired to a more intelligent and sophisticated way of living. When a new group forms, we share our past childhood conflicts and how those same conflicts are present in our current life (for example, our reenactments). While every situation is different we quickly see that some form of PTSD is present in all of our lives. We use our similarities to create a group of bonding and support. We meet weekly for two hours for 12 weeks. I find that 12 weeks of speaking, listening, writing and reading about concepts does a tremendous service to the re-wiring process. In between groups we use Google Chats or a private email link to offer support.

Here are a few excerpts from a recent chat:

Matt: "I think we are in a better place in our marriage than we have been in years. I think the 20 concepts have played a big part in helping us establish some healthier boundaries. I've been using them at work too and have decided to change jobs. I don't have to participate in that dysfunctional system and it's not my duty to rescue that place."

Lynn: "Great to hear about your relationship and job Matt. I have been doing really well too. I'm no longer afraid of my feelings but I "feel" them and honestly, modulation has given me power and confidence in ways I didn't know possible."

Shari: "I continue to struggle as a single mom and I remind myself that adult responsibility is non-negotiable. I also take adult responsibility for my own little child inside me. Ellie, be aware of attachment issues regarding your relationship. Also, I see loyalty to the perpetrator and re-enactments! Sorry, just being honest…you know I care! Modulate like crazy to keep your rational thinking brain active! I'm working on modulation myself right now!"

Ellie: "Thanks Shari! I appreciate your honesty. I am working on brain/body, attachment, magical thinking and modulation. I think one of my favorite concepts is the thinking/feeling/behavior loop…using it for positive instead of telling myself scary stories. I have to stop looking at my partner as a perpetrator and myself as a victim. The new guy is just a rescuer and I'm not showing adult responsibility in any way."

Peter: "Sorry I have been out of the chats. It looks like everyone is doing a great job re-wiring! I continue to stay clean and sober going to meetings. I want to end this miserable situation with my relationship. I think it is another addiction. There is definitely magical thinking going on when I tell myself I can change her. I'm practicing locus of control, knowing I didn't do anything wrong to make this happen and I can't do anything to fix her. I can just be honest and use the 5-part-formula to tell her my thoughts, feelings and what I want. The rest is up to her. Can't wait to see you all next week!"

Ellie: "I will offer a potluck at my house before group, who's in?"

As I was writing this, yet another example came in on my phone:

A client is struggling in her relationship. She believes her significant other is frequently dominating the conversation, acting more like a parent/teacher than an equal partner in their relationship. She writes that she intends to use the concepts to address her thoughts, feelings and desires. Here is the feedback from Marla, another group member:

Marla: "Hey Jax, thanks for reaching out to the group. What I heard in your check-in was your decision to stay out of the victim/perpetrator/ rescuer triangle regarding your situation with Karen. Adult responsibility on board and your willingness to tolerate the discomfort of doing things differently will help a lot! I will caution you about your saying/thinking "how hard it's going to be." That's a scary story you're telling yourself and it pulls you right into the thinking/feeling/behavior loop in a negative direction. Stay anchored, take deep breaths and possibly ask her to hear you rather than try to fix you. Use modulation, desensitization and remember that her reactions are her own. Locus of control tells us that we can only control ourselves, so let that be your focus! Integration is the concept that will work here! Please let us know how this all works out!"

Can you see how powerful a group of "like-minded" people can be in helping with the re-wiring?

Share this book with another person, a friend, sibling, daughter or son, and talk to them about it. Use The 20 Concepts to understand problems and address them using these healthy solutions. I have found that couples develop profound intimacy when *both* people are using these tools to navigate their relationship. Read the book with your partner if you have one and notice how the relationship begins to improve immediately.

Another excellent and effective way to re-wire is to start a 20 Concepts book group and meet regularly, no less than monthly. Add an online or Google Chat group to offer support in-between meetings, as you read about previously. Repetition (speaking, hearing, reading, and writing) creates hardwiring.

Brain re-wiring isn't easy, but it isn't as hard as living life in a regressive way, repeating the same dramatic (and dysfunctional) patterns again and again! Now that you know how… It's just a matter of integrating these concepts and tolerating the discomfort of thinking, feeling and behaving differently. The more you practice these concepts in all your affairs, the more consciously you will live.

ASK YOURSELF

Now that I know "how to" re-wire my brain; why wouldn't I?

SIX

Grief and Loss

GRIEF AND LOSS

The Things that Didn't Happen, that Should Have

This book is incomplete without a chapter on grief and loss. We have all experienced it at some point in our lives. Many of us reading this book will have experienced it deeply due to what *didn't* happen in our childhood. We often examine the things that happened, that shouldn't have, such as abuse, confusion and neglect. Now it's time to look at the "things that didn't happen, that should have."

We *should* have been safe, held and had a consistent, predictable loving home life. We *needed* our parents to be healthy role models and demonstrate what a loving healthy relationship looks like between two parents. We *deserved* support, involvement (not too much or too little), and we needed to hear that we mattered, that we were wanted and adored. We should have had discipline (not punishment), guidance, and thoughtful consequences appropriate to our age and behavior. It was so very important to be taught guidelines and limits so that we could develop a healthy moral compass for ourselves. Our parents should have given us all of this and more. Their job was to provide more than food and shelter. But… You can't give, what you don't have. And truth be told, most of our parents didn't get these things from their parents either. While that can explain why, it doesn't take away the fact that there was something vital missing in our childhood and we "feel" that loss. All of us who have had attachment conflicts most likely have tremendous, unexpressed, and therefore unresolved grief and loss.

Dr. Elizabeth Kubler-Ross wrote a book in 1969 titled, *On Death and Dying* in which she outlines that there are specific phases to the grief and loss process. During my 30 years of practice, I have seen all of those phases present whenever anyone comes to see mc who has experienced a loss, no matter what that loss was. The process is the same whether someone has literally died, a relationship has ended, or if there is *any* type of loss. I will explain the latter in more detail soon.

The phases as written by Ross are Denial, Anger, Bargaining, Depression and Acceptance. In the 40 plus years since that publication, I have found that the phases have shifted slightly. This is how I use them… Shock and Denial, Bargaining, Anger and Pain, Acceptance, and Moving on. Going through these stages is not a smooth transition from one into the other. Sometimes we will go back and forth from one phase to another. Often if we refuse to experience a phase, our process stops and we become stuck; which means we may never really get over the loss. Many people will deny that they feel anger when a loss has occurred, especially if the loss is the death of a loved one. These people can stay embedded in the pain, which will affect all their relationships to some degree.

If we deny the grief and loss process completely; then whenever there is loss, it's likely that we will experience, not just the current loss, but also all the unexpressed losses of the past. This could cause what is called emotional flooding and that can be dangerous. Because emotional flooding will impair our judgment, we may believe that we can't tolerate such pain and suicidal ideation or some other form of self-harm could take over in order to escape the feelings of such deep sorrow and despair.

Let's gently and with compassion for ourselves look at the phases of grief and loss when the loss was not having the parents we always wanted and needed. It's so important to have a heartfelt awareness that there is *tremendous* loss due to neglect and/or abuse. For those of us who lost our childhood innocence due to sexual abuse, we ache in an additional way.

Below, I point out how to use the concepts to assist in the grief and loss process:

Shock and Denial

Many of my clients are shocked when I tell them that they may have PTSD and they are quick to deny that there was abuse or neglect in their childhood. Yet, the events that they are describing to me are an obvious contradiction to that denial. There are three concepts that could be helpful here. The first is *Concept 1: Understanding Your Brain and Body*. Recall that with a little underdeveloped brain we aren't able to understand that what is happening is neglect or abuse, therefore it is understandable that as an adult we are surprised and sometimes defensive. Next, consider another concept, *Concept 2: Attachment* – remembering that as a child the need for survival was to attach… no matter what! Even if that meant we created a magical story of pretending things were different than they really were. As adults we often hold onto that magical thinking. More denial comes from *Concept 4: Locus of Control* – such as I deserved it, I was no angel, or I had it coming. Can you hear how we can take responsibility for our parents' behavior? Yet, the truth is we never could control what our parents did or did not do.

Bargaining

Bargaining statements can be heard as, "If I had done things differently… it would have been different". Again, *Concept 4: Locus of Control* can be seen here. Comments such as "If my mother didn't have to work so much" or "If my father wasn't so abused as a child" distract us from the fact that whatever the reason for the neglect or abuse, accepting it *did* happen and having compassion for yourself is the way through this process. You can have understanding and compassion for your parents later. But this is *your* process to healing, now!

Something I also hear from clients is "My parents had it worse than I did"; which is just another form of bargaining, minimizing what did or did not happen to you. Concept 4 reminds us that we didn't make anything happen or not happen. We really never had that control. We also were not bad or wrong. We were small helpless children.

Anger and Pain

The feeling of anger is always present when we are abused; it is a physiological response that we can't stop. Yet, as children it often wasn't safe to express our anger so we acted it out in other ways. Many adults are still very uncomfortable being angry with their parents. Deep loyalty issues are embedded here. This suppressed anger can get expressed in intimate relationships, as well as with bosses, teachers, therapists or anyone who even slightly resembles any type of authority figure. This will sabotage all attempts at healthy relationships. It is helpful to be angry at what did or did not happen; not at the people who were so unskilled and harmful.

Remember that whenever there is anger, there is also pain. It is tremendously painful to be neglected and/or to be unable to form healthy, secure, loving attachments with our parents. Sometimes a person is more comfortable with expressing anger and becomes furious seeing their parents as entirely evil, which can be a way to avoid feeling the pain of such loss. Perhaps a person can only be comfortable expressing sadness over what didn't happen, while refusing to experience or express anger. These two emotions have been misunderstood for decades and it's time to embrace the fact that both feelings exist and need to be expressed. We don't need to express them to our parents; we can discharge these emotions by discussing them with friends, in therapy, and/or in a support group. Journaling, crying...yelling out loud when alone, can all be helpful ways to discharge this energy from the body.

We can use the following concepts to assist us in this stage:

Concept 12: Feel our Feelings – Allowing ourselves to embrace that we have these feelings and that it's normal and natural, not only to *feel* them but to *express* them as well.

Concept 19: Tolerating the Discomfort – It can be very uncomfortable feeling and expressing ourselves this way, however it's important to re-mind ourselves that our feelings won't harm us but holding them in, very likely will.

Concept 16: Modulation – Trusting that we can have a gentle conversation with ourselves while feeling, and not letting ourselves lose control. We can increase or decrease our emotions through thoughts of compassion for ourselves, *and* understanding that our abusers were likely victims themselves.

Concept 18: Integration – Helping us to understand that it doesn't have to be an either/or when it comes to anger and pain in this situation, meaning that both can be present at the same time.

Acceptance and Moving On

Accepting that you didn't have a healthy physical and/or emotionally safe childhood can be difficult. There occasionally can be some form of shame attached to this. I believe it has to do with *Locus of Control* issues; that somehow *you* were the one who made these bad things happen or that you weren't lovable for some reason. Of course this is not true. You were a perfectly wonderful little being who was completely dependent on your parents to reflect back to you that you were important and lovable and that you mattered! When we accept what happened and didn't happen, we become integrated. When we allow ourselves to feel our anger and our pain, we become integrated. When we are fragmented we continue to suffer and when integrated we can move on.

In addition to *Locus of Control* and *Integration* – the concept that supports this part of the grief and loss process is the *Thinking/Feeling/Behavior Loop* – having intelligent thought about what happened while embracing and holding our feelings gently will assist us in moving through the world in a kind and loving way. Being aware that the story we tell ourselves over and over will affect our feelings and our behavior will follow. My true story is: I was hurt and confused. I did the best I could as a small child and still I suffered a great loss. That hurts! And… I'm angry that life can seem so unfair! I'm also angry that my parents were so unhealthy! I'm going to be like a parent to myself now. The kind of parent I didn't have… I'll speak respectfully to myself and make sure all of my needs are met. I'll love myself and celebrate life. It's over now! I'll walk with grace, dignity and kindness; realizing that so many people I come in contact with in my life may also be suffering from similar loss.

Lastly, *Concept 20: Adult Responsibility is Non-Negotiable* – which tells us that suppressing feelings and avoiding this process locks us into a regressive position and that our behavior will reflect that. The ability to respond to life's losses with the maturity of intelligent and compassionate thoughts and behaviors will make moving on a meaningful experience.

If you have not done grief and loss work around your childhood abuse or neglect it could be helpful to find a therapist to guide you through this process, as it can be very emotional. There are also excellent grief and loss support groups available. You don't have to do this alone!

Through embarking on and moving through each phase of the grief and loss process we can develop a profound compassion and empathy for ourselves. This is how we heal. We, as adults must hold *ourselves* (child, adolescent, teen and young adult) with a gentleness and love that guides us through all of our life's endeavors.

SEVEN

A Promising Future

A PROMISING FUTURE

A Hidden Agenda

A promise is to make a declaration that something will or will not happen! It's a reassurance that an expectation will be met. The word promise is not a word to be used lightly!

I will make *you* a promise and it is this…If you use these 20 Concepts in all of your affairs, you *will* be happier and more at peace in your life. And isn't that what we all want? To be happier and more satisfied most of the time; to love and be loved; to have a sense of adventure and playfulness and to have our lives really matter? Of course, there will be challenges along the way; I can also promise you that! We will have intense feelings and sometimes angry thoughts in the face of those struggles and yet, it's important to remember to integrate the concepts during those moments as well. What comes to mind is a line I heard somewhere long ago that states, "It's not *what* happens in life that matters, it's *how you deal* with what happens that really matters". To have an intelligent, kind and graceful response to life's many challenges is what the use of The 20 Concepts offers. Remember, living a life of grace, intelligence and dignity are the end results of this work.

The 20 Concepts promise even more than the above paragraph. When used consistently they offer a fun, adventurous, celebration of life.

This isn't magical thinking! Brain re-wiring is based on the most recent and advanced scientific research. It not only has a profound effect on recovery from PTSD; it has the potential to assist you in *any* and *all* of your endeavors, and in living the kind of life you want to live.

As I watched, my own visions begin to manifest into reality. Living in this new, conscious, intelligent and abundant way became an exciting lifestyle. "Live Large!" I tell my clients, "Live a BIG life!" Think about how you want that life to look… Who will be there? What will you be doing? How will you feel? Envision all the details! Can you see where to start, how to proceed and where you will end up?

Ralph Waldo Emerson once said, "If one advances confidently in the directions of his dreams and endeavors to live the life which he has imagined, he will meet with a success unexpected in common hours."

Once re-wired, you become less focused on painful memories and more focused on creating. Another way of putting it is to say that as the activity in our survival brain decreases and we are calmer, the activity in the creative part of the brain is increased and we are more aware. This allows one to "become more of who one is, authentically; and to become everything that one is capable of becoming," which is an inspiring quote from the highly respectable Abraham Maslow, who dedicated his life to an approach for living called "Self-Actualization." The result of using his approach was described as "reaching exalted states of awareness and living." He went on to say that "Just living this way makes a tremendous contribution to all one comes in contact with, as well as the world one lives in."

Now we come to the hidden agenda, which can also be seen as another benefit to re-wiring and evolving your brain. Many of us have heard the words, "Collective Consciousness" yet what does that really mean?

Well, certainly after reading this book we all know the difference between unconscious and conscious thinking! So, collective consciousness means, many people being awake, aware and conscious at the same time. Another way of explaining this is to look at Quantum Physics. Now, I warn you that Quantum Physics is no easy study, but if you are curious, then just Google the words and you will get a basic understanding of the relationship between Quantum Physics and collective consciousness. This is what Maslow is referring to in the previous paragraph regarding how we contribute to the entire world, just by living with awareness!

The 20 Concepts teach us how to achieve this ability to contribute. I'm positive about this because I have been doing it for years! I did it with *intention*; I was very clear how I intended to live. I added *motivation*; the same old patterns and disappointments were unacceptable! I was done!! And then I knew that there had to be more than me just getting what I wanted. When I saw the *purpose* behind doing this work, it became a passion. The purpose was to make a contribution to humankind, to evolve my own brain in order to help evolve the human species – Less violence and stupidity! More love, kindness and abundance. We are more generous when we truly have all (and even more) of what we need. Can we each contribute to the obliteration of child abuse, child neglect, sexual abuse, and war? I say, "Yes, we can" and "Let it begin with me!"

EIGHT

From My Library to Yours

FROM MY LIBRARY TO YOURS

"With Knowledge; Comes Power"

Istarted my quest for knowledge regarding the human body, mind, spirit and soul over 50 years ago. I longed to understand the workings of the universe and what, as humans, our existence was all about. I most likely will continue to research and learn for many more years to come.

I want to share with you some of the very best thinkers and writers that I have had the pleasure of reading. Please open your minds and explore the world of great and profound thought.

The Developing Mind by Daniel Sicgcl MD

A Users Guide to the Brain by John Ratey MD

Molecules of Emotion by Candice Pert

Psycho-Cybernetics by Maxwell Maltz MD

Change your Brain Change your Life by Dr. Daniel Amen

The Trauma Model by Colin Ross MD

Traumatic Stress by Bessell van der Kolk MD

Healing Trauma by Peter Levine PhD

Betrayal Trauma by Jennifer J Freyd

Necessary Losses by Judith Viorst

General Theory of Love by Thomas Lewis

Primal Wound by Nancy Newton Verrier

The Grief Recovery Handbook by J. James and R. Friedman

Healing the Shame that Binds You by John Bradshaw

Changing Course by Claudia Black

Co Dependent No More by Melody Beattie

Your Erroneous Zones by Dr. Wayne Dyer

I'm OK—You're OK by Thomas Harris MD

Creative Visualizations by Shaki Gawain

The Power of Now by Ekhart Tolle

The Four Agreements by Don Miquel Ruiz

The 7 Habits of Highly Effective People by Steven Covey

Evolutionaries by Carter Phipps

NINE

An Invitation